D1180465

OXFORD UNITED
Miscellany

OXFORD UNITED
Miscellany

*Oxford United Trivia,
History, Facts & Stats*

MARTIN BRODETSKY

OXFORD UNITED
Miscellany

All statistics, facts and figures are correct as of 5th May 2010

Published By:
Pitch Publishing (Brighton) Ltd
A2 Yeoman Gate
Yeoman Way
Durrington
BN13 3QZ

Email: info@pitchpublishing.co.uk
Web: www.pitchpublishing.co.uk

First published 2010

10-digit ISBN: 1-9054118-1-2
13-digit ISBN: 978-1-9054118-1-8

Printed and bound in Great Britain by Berforts Group

FOREWORD BY KELVIN THOMAS

I am delighted to have been asked to write a few words for this new book which looks at so many of the facts and random stories surrounding Oxford United. Most clubs have a colourful history and I think Oxford United have experienced a great deal of highs and lows since they were first formed as Headington FC.

From the early days as 'The Boys from up the Hill', to the building of the Manor Ground, the famous cup runs of the sixties and the glories of the eighties, the club has built up a history, plus several heroes and characters, who have become part of Oxford United folklore.

Martin has always had an eye for the quirkier side of football and it has been very entertaining to flick through these pages and fill in some of the gaps in our chequered past.

I think as a club we need to be proud of our past while also looking to the future as well. I firmly believe that we are heading in the right direction on and off the pitch and there are bright times ahead. In a few years' time a whole generation of new names will be added to the likes of Atkinson, Aldridge and Houghton and they will take their place in the pantheon of Oxford's greats.

Enjoy the book as we look forward to the exciting new chapters that lie ahead of us.

Kelvin Thomas
Chairman, Oxford United Football Club

INTRODUCTION

In forty-plus years of watching the soap opera that is Oxford United, I've come to realise that many of the characters and plots are too far-fetched to be believable. If the United drama were a work of art, would it be considered surrealism, Dadaism, or possibly faux-naiveté? Or Cubism, perhaps?

Conducting research into this book has been a positive pleasure, digging up some of the more abstruse facts and being inundated with bizarre anecdotes by practically everyone I've spoken to. Some of them were, sadly, too obscure or personal even for this volume, but what I hope I've been able to compile will be interesting, informative, and quirky enough to satisfy everyone.

I am lucky in that I have a reasonable collection of United programmes and other ephemera going back to the start of the professional era of the club. This has helped enormously in compiling this book, as has the newspaper archive at the Oxfordshire Studies Centre at Westgate Library in Oxford and, of course, the large number of people I've spoken to who have been involved with the club over many decades.

In particular, I'd like to thank Oxford's chairman Kelvin Thomas for agreeing to write the foreword, general manager Mick Brown for taking the time to discuss many of the behind-the-scenes activities, and communications officer Chris Williams for help above and beyond the call of duty.

Others whom it would be remiss of me not to thank include Ian Pearce for his invaluable IT skills, Dave Crabtree and Mark Gardener for their insights into the Oxford music scene, Peter Tickler for discussing his oeuvre, and too many others to name individually who have allowed me access to snippets of their past. In addition I would like to thank my editor, Dan Tester, and all at Pitch for their hard work and advice.

Last, but by no means least, thanks to Alison for her unstinting support and encouragement, and the kids (Dom, Jason, Rachel, Anna, and Lucy) for their constant interruptions and reminders that there are more important things in life than Oxford United Football Club.

Martin Brodetsky

WHAT THE DOCTOR ORDERED

OXFORD United were formed as Headington FC on Friday 27th October 1893, at a meeting called by Dr Robert Hitchings at the Britannia Inn, on London Road, Headington. Dr Hitchings, who lived in Windmill Road, was captain of the Headington United Cricket Club and, with the cricket season over, he wanted to provide the young men of the parish with something to occupy themselves over the winter months. Dr Hitchings also played for the new club, scoring in their second recorded game, a 3-3 draw with Victoria, on January 13th 1894. Many of the football club's earliest players were also members of the cricket club, whose ground they shared from 1925 until 1949.

A DOCTOR IN THE HOUSE

DR Hitchings wasn't the only medical man to play for the club. Ceri Evans came to Oxford from New Zealand to study as a Rhodes Scholar, gaining a first-class honours degree in experimental psychology. Richard Hill, who had played in New Zealand after he left Leicester City, knew of Evans, who was an established New Zealand international centre-back, and he suggested that Oxford gave him a trial. After he retired from professional football Evans became a locum in London – and played for Marlow – but missed their FA Cup win over Oxford in November 1994 through injury. He eventually returned 'down under' to become a forensic psychiatrist in Christchurch.

BLOOMING FOREIGNERS

OXFORD have fielded many non-British/Irish players. The earliest recorded was Brian 'Bud' Houghton, who was born in Madras, India, the son of a major in the Indian Army. In 1979, Dominican-born Joe Cooke joined United from Bradford, and Mark Stein – from Cape Town – joined Oxford from QPR in 1988, followed by Ceri Evans the following year. The next players of non-UK origin arrived in 1997, when Surinamese defender Brian Wilsterman was signed from Beerschott for £200,000, shortly followed by French defender Christophe Remy and Dutch goalie Arjan van Heusden. Foreign keepers were all the rage in 1999, when Andre Arendse and Pål Lundin vied for the number one shirt. A plethora of foreign players followed, particularly under the management of Argentine Ramon Díaz, while Latvian international Kristaps Grebis was signed by Jim Smith in 2007.

THE BIG SCREEN

IT was very rare for non-league sides to be featured on British Pathé. The media company was founded by Charles Pathé in Paris in the 1890s, became established in London in 1902, and by 1910 was producing a bi-weekly cinematic newsreel. Headington United appeared on the February 4th 1954 release, which showed their FA Cup fourth round tie against Bolton Wanderers, which the First Division side won 4-2 five days earlier. Oxford were also featured in further FA Cup games when, under the title 'Oxford Superb', they beat Blackburn Rovers 3-1 in the FA Cup fifth round, in footage issued on February 20th 1964, five days after the match. They were shown again two weeks later when they lost 2-1 to Preston North End in the FA Cup quarter-final. The heading for this feature was 'Out go Oxford'. Pathé stopped producing their newsreel in 1970. United's game against Blackburn was also shown on BBC's *Sports Special* in that programme's final broadcast on February 15th 1964, with Wally Barnes doing the commentary. This programme was the forerunner of *Match of the Day*, and was the first programme on television to feature regular Football League highlights. It began broadcasting in October 1955, but by the time Oxford appeared the programme was outmoded and was being phased out, with only highlights from FA Cup games being shown in its final season.

THE LITTLE SCREEN

The Real Eddie English was a four-episode TV thriller set in Oxford and filmed by Channel 4. The cast included Frank Windsor and Beryl Cook. Apart from its location, this 1989 drama is of interest to Oxford supporters because scenes for one episode were filmed at the Manor, during United's 2-0 FA Cup third round replay win over Sunderland on January 11th 1989. *The Manageress*, starring Cherie Lunghi and Warren Clarke, was first broadcast in the same year and featured a fictional game that was filmed at the Manor. The screenplay for this was written by Stan Hey, who also wrote a series devised by Gary Lineker, called *All in the Game*, starring Lloyd Owen and Warren Clarke (again). This was made by ITV in 1993; the small club where the star began his career was based at the Manor, which featured in the first two episodes (out of six).

MATCHES OF THE DAY

OXFORD United were featured 15 times on BBC's national *Match of the Day*, before the formation of the Premiership in 1992 changed the nature of television's football coverage. In the programme's first season, Oxford's game against Tranmere Rovers at the Manor on January 9th 1965 was the first game from outside Division One to be shown; Cyril Beavon's penalty gave United a 1-0 win over the Division Four leaders. United were also featured the following season, although this time their game at Oldham on May 21st ended in a 3-0 defeat. In 1968/69 United featured twice on *MOTD*, with different conclusions; on September 14th goals from Graham Atkinson and John Shuker gave the U's a 2-1 win at Sheffield United to end the Blades' 100% home record, but on February 8th Oxford were hammered 5-0 at Cardiff City. On November 21st 1970 the BBC must have regretted sending its cameras to cover United's 0-0 draw with Swindon Town, from which Graham Atkinson's long-range shot against the bar was the only highlight worth showing. United's FA Cup fifth round tie at Leicester City, which ended 1-1, was shown on February 13th 1971. The 1-0 win over Manchester United in Division Two on February 8th 1975 was Oxford's next showing, and the *Match of the Day* cameras also visited Oxford on December 3rd 1977, when a Peter Foley goal earned a 1-1 draw with Shrewsbury Town in a Third Division encounter. United were still in Division Three on September 29th 1979, when the programme showed first-placed Sheffield United beating second-placed Oxford 3-1, and on January 9th 1982, when the U's lost 2-0 at Huddersfield Town. Oxford were shown three times during the 1984/85 season, as they marched to the Second Division title. On November 24th, a John Aldridge hat-trick and goals from Gary Briggs and Billy Hamilton were enough to beat Leeds United 5-2, in a game marred by Leeds supporters dismantling a TV gantry and throwing bits of it onto the pitch. On February 23rd Oxford drew 1-1 at Blackburn Rovers, and on April 20th, the cameras captured another 5-2 victory, and another Aldridge hat-trick, as United beat Oldham Athletic. Oxford were next shown on February 28th 1988, when their 2-0 defeat at Luton Town in the Littlewoods Cup semi-final second leg was broadcast live. United's final showing was on January 26th 1991, when they lost their fourth round FA Cup tie 4-2 at Tottenham Hotspur, Martin Foyle's double not enough to overcome Paul Gascoigne's genius.

AUNTIE IN THE REGIONS

IN the 1969/70 season, the BBC showed regional matches after the main *Match of the Day* offering. Oxford were shown three times in this slot, with BBC Wales broadcasting United's 1-1 home draw with Cardiff City on November 15th. The same region also showed the return match on March 28th, a 0-0 draw at Ninian Park. The following week, on April 4th, viewers in the Midlands region were shown the 1-1 draw between Oxford and Charlton Athletic at the Manor.

SUNDAY AFTERNOONS ON THE BOX

THE 1968/69 season, United's first in Division Two, saw Oxford feature in the first season of *Star Soccer*. On November 2nd, the ATV cameras captured a Graham Atkinson goal securing a 1-0 win at Birmingham City. Oxford also appeared on January 30th 1971, when they lost 2-1 at home to Sheffield United. On August 28th 1971 *Star Soccer* showed Oxford's 2-1 win over Burnley, and on August 26th 1972 United's 2-1 defeat at Nottingham Forest was the featured game. Later that season the show broadcast another 2-1 defeat, at Aston Villa on March 31st. United next appeared on October 11th 1975, when Brian Heron broke his leg in a 1-0 win at Notts County. The final Oxford game on *Star Soccer* was a 0-0 draw at Shrewsbury Town on March 24th 1979. London Weekend Television first showed United on their *The Big Match* on September 7th 1968, when a John Evanson goal gave the U's a 1-0 win over Fulham. Another Oxford game shown by LWT was a 1-0 win over Sunderland on September 15th 1973. Other ITV channels that showed Oxford included Granada, who featured United on their *Kick Off Match* on February 2nd 1974 when Blackpool won 2-0, on April 13th 1974 for a goalless draw at Preston, and on November 2nd 1974 for United's 4-0 defeat at Manchester United. On September 9th 1972, United's 1-0 defeat at Huddersfield Town was broadcast by Yorkshire Television, who also showed United's 1-0 win at Sheffield Wednesday on November 24th 1973. *Shoot*, broadcast by Tyne Tees TV, featured United's 3-0 defeat at Sunderland on February 12th 1972, a 2-0 defeat at Roker Park on October 5th 1974, and a 1-0 defeat at the same venue on December 13th 1975. HTV's *Soccer Special* showed highlights of Oxford's 2-0 defeat at Bristol City on April 12th 1969.

THE Southern network featured Oxford losing 3-0 at Portsmouth on October 5th 1968, but made up for that by showing United's 2-0 win at Fratton Park on November 29th 1975. In January 1982, ATV was replaced by Central TV. The rebranded company's first Oxford game on *Star Soccer* was the 4-0 fourth round FA Cup defeat at Coventry City on February 13th. On October 16th 1982, the programme showed highlights of Oxford's 4-2 win over Walsall. ITV cameras were at the Manor on December 19th 1983 for United's Milk Cup fourth-round second-replay 2-1 win over Manchester United. On February 18th 1984, *The Big Match* featured highlights of United's FA Cup fifth round 3-0 home defeat by Sheffield Wednesday. The LWT cameras were at Fellows Park on April 7th 1984 for United's 1-0 win over Walsall, and they also showed highlights of United's 1-0 defeat at Manchester City on October 6th 1984 and the 2-1 'Santa Claus' defeat at Portsmouth on December 22nd. In a bad season for the U's on *The Big Match*, the programme also featured United's 1-0 defeat at Leeds on April 27th. United's first season in the top flight was marred by a dispute between the TV companies and the Football League, with no games broadcast until January 1986. Some games were covered by ITV for transmission overseas, including Oxford's 1-1 home draw with Luton Town on October 22nd and the 4-3 comeback win over Ipswich on November 23rd 1985, but they couldn't be shown on British TV, while the 4-2 win over Luton on December 6th 1986 was also covered by ITV crews for screening abroad. Once the dispute was resolved, United featured on *The Big Match* on January 8th 1986, when highlights of United's 2-1 defeat at Spurs in an FA Cup third round replay were shown. Central were due to cover United's Milk Cup semi-final first leg at Aston Villa on February 11th, but the game was postponed to March 4th, when the 2-2 draw was broadcast exclusively on Central. ITV broadcast Oxford's Milk Cup final win over QPR live on Sunday 20th April 1986, and six days later ITV showed highlights of United's 3-2 defeat at Ipswich. They made up for it four days later when they broadcast highlights of the U's beating Everton 1-0. Oxford featured just once the following season, when LWT and Granada showed highlights of the Yellows' 3-1 defeat at Tottenham on April 25th 1987. On February 6th 1988, the LWT cameras captured United's incredible 7-4 defeat at Luton Town.

MONEY FOR NOTHING

ON Saturday 27th February 1999, Oxford played Sunderland at the Manor in the first pay-per-view match shown live on British television. The game, which had a 6.00pm kick-off, was an uneventful goalless draw with an attendance of 9,044, boosted by an estimated 50,000 television viewers paying Sky £7.95 on top of their normal Sky subscription.

THERE'S ONLY ONE UNITED

ACTUALLY, there were at least four other clubs called Oxford United. Two of them played in Northern Ireland, but Lurgan-based Oxford United, who played in the Mid-Ulster Football League, merged with Sunnyside FC in October 2002 and changed their name to Oxford-Sunnyside. Oxford were formed in Lurgan in the mid-1970s and won five Junior Cup titles; they were the top team in the Mid-Ulster Football League for around 14 years. The other Ulster-based club carrying the Oxford moniker is the Oxford United Stars, based in Derry and competing in the Northern Ireland Intermediate League. They are known as the U2s in reference to Oxford United's nickname 'The U's', and they even purloined United's badge of the late 1990s, although their colours are blue and black stripes. A third Oxford United exists in Gambia; they won the 2009 Gunjur Nawettan league championship tournament, beating Nyokoyorr 5-4 on penalties in the final after a 1-1 draw. In Barbados there's another Oxford United, who played in the semi-finals of the Massive Promotions Checker Hall Out-Of-Season Football Tournament in December 2006. Alas, I could find no record of their progress in that superbly named competition.

QUICK START

OXFORD'S fastest home goal was scored by Jamie Lambert after 17 seconds, against Colchester on November 2nd 1999 in a 1-1 draw; three seconds quicker than Geoff Denial's opener in Headington's 3-0 win over Poole Town on February 27th 1960. Tcham N'Toya scored after 47 seconds when Oxford beat Barnet 2-0 on April 15th 2006. Away from home, Phil Gray scored after ten seconds of United's 4-3 defeat at Bournemouth on April 3rd 2001, while on September 12th 1983, Andy Thomas scored within the opening 16 seconds of a 1-0 League Cup win at Bristol City.

ONE BRIEF SHOT AT GLORY

THERE have been many players whose Oxford career has been short, but ten players have made just one substitute appearance before disappearing into obscurity. Diminutive winger Tony Obi famously played for just 15 minutes in a First Division match at Watford in the first game of the 1986/87 season, while another player fitting the same description, Doudou (full name Ebeli Mbombo Doudou, Ramon Díaz's first signing), played the second half at Bury in January 2005 before having to return to his native Congo for family reasons. Canadian goalkeeper Hubert Busby Junior played for the second half at Wycombe in September 2000 in a game shown live on Sky, saving a penalty. Unfortunately, the linesman decided that he'd moved too early, and he was unable to repeat the save with the retaken spot kick. Scot Gemmill's contribution to United's attempts to avoid relegation to the Conference in 2006 lasted just 17 minutes at Mansfield Town – during which time the Stags scored the only goal of the game – before he decided he'd had enough and left for New Zealand; surely the furthest anyone has travelled to avoid playing for the Yellows? Other players who can claim this distinction are Stuart Gibson (who came off the bench in an Associate Members Cup game at Swindon Town), Josh Kennet (who replaced Rufus Brevett in a Conference game at Exeter City), Paul Milsom, Marcus Phillips, Ryan Semple, and Mark Stevens. However, even Obi's 15 minutes seems an age compared with Abdou Sall's Oxford career. Sall, on loan from Kidderminster Harriers, made his debut in United's FA Cup second-round win over Swindon, coming on with just five seconds of stoppage time remaining. He also came on as substitute for Jefferson Louis in United's next game, at Bristol Rovers, where he played for the last five minutes. In neither appearance did Sall touch the ball.

FIRST OFF THE BENCH

THE law permitting the use of a substitute in competitive games was introduced in 1965. The first time Oxford took advantage of the new ruling was on September 18th 1965, when Alan Willey replaced Tony Jones in a 3-1 defeat at Bristol Rovers. The first Oxford United substitute to score was Tony Buck, who found the net in a 2-1 League Cup first-round defeat at Peterborough on August 24th 1966, after he replaced John Evanson.

LIVE AND DANGEROUS

OXFORD United have featured in live televised games 47 times (excluding those shown only overseas). Their first live match was the Milk Cup final on April 20th 1986, shown on ITV, followed two years later by the Littlewoods Cup semi-final defeat at Luton Town, on the BBC. Oxford's first league game to be televised live was a Division One game at Swindon on September 20th 1992, which ended 2-2. This was on ITV, as was the 1-0 win at Derby County the following month. The first game to be televised live at the Manor was a 0-0 draw with Leicester City on December 13th 1992, also on ITV. The first time that Oxford featured on Sky was September 8th 1996, when United lost 2-0 at Reading, while a 0-0 draw with Birmingham City on October 18th 1996 saw the Sky cameras at the Manor for the first time. The BBC cameras captured United's 1-0 win over Swindon Town in the FA Cup second round on December 8th 2002, which was the first time that a game was broadcast live from the Kassam Stadium. Ironically, United's relegation from the Football League resulted in them receiving a higher profile from the television companies, with Sky showing six Oxford games live in 2006/07, including both legs of the play-off semi-final against Exeter. The following season, Irish TV company Setanta won the rights to broadcast Conference matches, with the result that Oxford were shown eight times that season, with United failing to win any of them. Oxford's first win on Setanta came on September 23rd 2008, when they beat Cambridge United 3-1 at the Kassam. That was the third of nine Oxford games shown live that season, and the last time that the U's appeared live was the play-off final against York on May 16th 2010.

MORE PLAYERS THAN YOU CAN SHAKE A STICK AT

IN the 2007/08 season, United utilised a club record 41 different players, 19 of whom made fewer than half-a-dozen league starts, including goalkeepers Chris Tardif and Sam Warrell. Only three players appeared in more than 40 league games, with goalkeeper Billy Turley keeping 19 clean sheets in his 45 Conference appearances. Two seasons later, only five of the 41 players were still at the club (one of whom, Matt Green, had departed for Torquay United and later returned) including Turley.

SUBSTITUTE FOR ANOTHER GUY

THERE are some players whose destiny is to be a second string for someone else. Such as Matt Murphy, whose 91 substitute appearances are the most for an Oxford player, although he also made 191 starts for the club. Yemi Odubade came off the bench 71 times in 158 United appearances, while Chris Hackett found himself replacing other players in 63 games. Jamie Cook made more substitute appearances than starts in his first spell with Oxford. He started 40 games in the Football League, but was a playing substitute 53 times. Joey Beauchamp also made 53 substitute appearances, but compared with his 375 starts he wins the percentage game.

TAKEN OFF

WHILE Matt Murphy may have come off the bench more than any other Oxford player, he was also the second-most substituted player in Oxford's history, failing to finish 57 of the 191 games he started. Murphy also has the unenviable achievement of being a substitute who was later substituted; on April 16th 1996, United drew 1-1 with Notts County at the Manor, during which Murphy replaced Martin Aldridge. However, 27 minutes later Denis Smith took off Murphy for Martin Gray, a decision with which Murphy was not too happy. Murphy's failure to complete games pales into insignificance compared with Steve Basham's. The striker was substituted in 87 of his 157 starts. Joey Beauchamp was replaced on 47 occasions, while another local lad, Paul Powell, was taken off 44 times out of 160 starts.

LATIN SPIRIT

DESPITE the arrival of several South Americans during the reign of Argentine boss Ramon Díaz, they were not the first Latin Americans to play for Oxford. Díaz signed Uruguayan defender Mateo Corbo (whose ten bookings in 13 games must be a record), Argentine midfielders Lucas Cominelli and Juan Pablo Raponi, as well as his own sons Emiliano and Michael. These were all preceded by giant centre-back Brian Hank Wilsterman. Hailing from Paramaribo in the Dutch province of Suriname, he was signed from Belgian side Beerschot for £200,000 in March 1997. He stayed for two years before joining Rotherham United; his Hawaiian shirts and big smile almost made up for some appalling defending.

INTERNATIONAL MANAGERS

ALMOST everyone knows of Steve McClaren, the former Oxford midfielder who went on to manage England. However, he is not the only United connection who has become the manager of a national side. Mark Harrison was Malcolm Shotton's assistant, having played in goal for Port Vale, Stoke City, Kettering Town, Telford, and Stafford Rangers, whom he later managed. He also played for South African side Hellenic FC, with whom he was voted South African Goalkeeper of the Year. In March 2000 he was appointed coach of the Bangladesh side and given a three-year contract, moving from North Leigh to Dhaka to take charge of the national team during their World Cup qualifying campaign. Another former United player with national management connections is Dean Saunders, who has been Wales assistant manager since June 2007.

YOUNG GUNS

SINCE 1949, six players aged younger than 17 have played for the club. The youngest is Graham Atkinson, who was 16 years 108 days when he made his debut against Chelmsford on September 2nd 1959. Jason Seacole was 16 years 149 days when he came on as a substitute on September 7th 1976 against Mansfield Town. The player he replaced was Billy Jeffrey, who at that time held the record as United's youngest league player, being 16 years 336 days when he made his debut against Fulham, on September 26th 1973. United's third-youngest professional is Declan Benjamin, who came on as a substitute against Ebbsfleet on 17 November 2007 aged 16 years 286 days. Ben Weedon's debut was on January 28th 2006 at Rushden & Diamonds, aged 16 years 304 days. The most recent 16-year-old to play for United is Aaron Woodley, who came on as a substitute against Crawley on September 29th 2009, aged 16 years 352 days. All of these seem positively ancient compared with Jim Smith, who made his Headington United debut on April 2nd 1938, aged just 14 years. He scored in that game, a 7-3 win over Osberton Radiators in the Oxfordshire Senior League, and he was still a Headington United amateur when he retired in September 1955. Tony Harper was just 14½ when he played his first game for Headington after joining from Oxford City Colts in 1940. He moved to Brentford in 1948, and returned to United in 1955.

THE FOOT OF GOD

ONE of Headington's earliest known goalscorers, and a significant figure in the early development of the club, was the vicar of the local parish church, St. Andrews. The Reverend John Holford Scott-Tucker was Headington FC's first president and he was also a vice-president of the Oxford City Football Association, the first competition that Headington joined. At the age of 39 he played in the side's second known game, a 3-3 draw at home to Victoria on January 13th 1894. According to reports the Rev. Scott-Tucker "soon registered two goals by good rushes". Five years later, in July 1899, the Reverend Scott-Tucker was sued for bankruptcy after a strange affair when he stood surety for Mrs Kingscote, one of his parishioners, who borrowed over £50,000 from Lord Byron, a descendant of the famous poet. When Mrs Kingscote was declared bankrupt she fled to Switzerland, leaving the Reverend Scott-Tucker and George Moore, the vicar of Cowley (who had also stood surety), to pay the price of their naivety. He left the office of vicar of St. Andrews in June 1899, and with it relinquished the presidency of Headington FC, which he had held since the club's formation six years earlier.

OH, BROTHER

SINCE United turned professional, there have been a few brotherly pairings in the side. The most famous was Ron and Graham Atkinson, who both signed from Aston Villa in 1959. Over the next 13 seasons they played together in 321 games before joining up again at Kettering Town, where Ron had become manager. Goalkeeper Mick Kearns was the oldest of five brothers from Banbury and he made 78 appearances between 1970 and 1972, becoming the first home-grown Oxford player to win an international cap, for the Republic of Ireland; his younger brother Ollie played 23 games, but a decade later. Simon and Ross Weatherstone came up through the youth ranks, but only managed two first-team games together. Ben Weedon made his Oxford debut aged just 16, but his twin brother Chris didn't make the grade, while neither of the Tweed twins, James and Richard, appeared for the first team. Jamie Brooks made 53 appearances for United and was linked with a move to Arsenal before being struck down by Guillane-Barré Syndrome, while his brother Ryan failed to graduate beyond the youth team.

NO FATHER AND SON

IN modern times the club has never had a father and son on its books, although it has come close on a couple of occasions. Cyril Beavon was signed by Arthur Turner, making his debut on January 21st 1959. He went on to play 464 games for Oxford, seeing action in the Southern League and Divisions Four, Three, and Two of the Football League before leaving for Banbury United in the summer of 1969. Cyril's son Stuart was also a professional footballer, starting his career at Tottenham Hotspur but making his name at Reading. Stuart's son, also called Stuart (his father was actually named Michael Stuart Beavon) started his career with Ardley before moving to Wallingford, although it was while he was playing for Didcot Town that he came to wider attention, especially when he scored twice against AFC Sudbury in the 2005 final of the FA Vase at White Hart Lane. This performance earned Stuart a trial with Oxford, during which he scored in a 3-0 win over Swindon Town and played against Yeading, but he wasn't offered a contract and instead was signed by Weymouth, for whom he typically scored against Oxford on a couple of occasions. Tommy Caton joined Oxford from Arsenal in February 1987 and played 65 games for United over the next 15 months, before moving to Charlton Athletic. He died of a heart attack, aged just 30 years, on April 30th 1993. His son Andrew was five years old. In 2004 Andrew signed for Swindon Town as a first-year scholar. After failing to secure a regular first-team place, he was released by Swindon at Christmas 2007. In January 2008 he had a trial with Oxford United, playing against Milton United. However, he failed to follow in the footsteps of his father, and eventually signed for Team Bath. After they resigned from the Conference South he joined Oxford City in August 2009, but was released at the start of September, joining Weymouth.

BUNCH OF FIVES

SINCE United turned professional in 1949, only two players have scored five goals in a game. On December 10th 1960, Tony Jones went nap as United beat Wisbech 9-0, the club's biggest win since professionalism. Later that same season, on April 12th 1961, Bud Houghton hit five as the U's beat Boston United 7-2.

LEAPING ABOUT

SINCE 1893, United have played only twice on Leap Day, February 29th. Most recently, in 1992, a John Durnin goal secured a 1-1 draw at Blackburn Rovers. The earlier occasion, in 1964, was altogether more significant, as it marked the first time that a club from Division Four had reached the quarter-finals of the FA Cup. Having beaten First Division Blackburn 3-1 in the fifth round, United were drawn at home to Preston North End for the quarter-final. A record home crowd of 22,750 packed into the specially modified Manor Ground, and interest in the game was such that, for the first time for an Oxford fixture, a pirate programme was issued. Preston won 2-1, with Tony Jones scoring for Oxford in the second half. Despite their late pressure United were unable to get the replay they deserved and it was the Second Division club that met Swansea Town in the semi-final. Preston won that game 2-1, but lost in the final 3-2 to West Ham United.

LATE KICK-OFF

THE latest date on which United have played a competitive game was on June 1st, for an Oxford Hospital Cup semi-final tie against Pressed Steel at Oxford City's White House ground in 1940. Pressed Steel won 4-3, with Headington's goals coming from Jack Ramsden (2) and Charlie Machin. The latest date for a league match is May 28th, when United finished the 1965/66 season with a 3-0 home defeat by Scunthorpe United. This was five days later than the last game of the 1962/63 season, a 1-0 defeat at Newport County, and seven days later than United's 3-0 win at Pressed Steel at the end of the 1946/47 season, in Headington's last Oxfordshire Senior League match before they joined the Spartan League.

STUMPED

AFTER Headington Cricket Club vacated the Manor in 1949, the ground was solely used for football. That is, apart from on Tuesday 28th April 1981 when it hosted a cricket match between a Cherwell League XI and a Somerset County XI in support of Peter Denning's Benevolent Fund. This was a limited-overs game of 25 overs each, and was billed as the first floodlit cricket match in Oxfordshire.

EGGS FOR BREAKFAST

THE Kassam Stadium has hosted four significant rugby union matches. On April 27th 2002, a crowd of 7,882 saw London Irish meet Pontypridd in the Parker Pen Shield semi-final, with the Welsh side winning 33-27 to set up a final against Sale Sharks, also held at the Kassam Stadium, on May 26th 2002. This game was won 25-22 by Sale, with 12,000 in attendance. On May 21st 2005, Sale Sharks were back in Oxford to play Section Paloise in the European Challenge Cup final (the Parker Pen sponsorship having ended), with Sale again triumphant, beating the French side 27-3 in a game watched by a crowd of 7,230. This game formed part of a double-header with the final of the European Shield, between French side FC Auch and Worcester Warriors, with Auch winning 23-10 in front of a crowd of 2,823.

NEUTRAL GROUND

BOTH the Manor and the Kassam Stadium have hosted football matches that haven't involved Oxford. In the 1950s the Manor took over from Oxford City's White House ground as the preferred venue for Oxfordshire Senior Cup finals, having previously been used as a neutral semi-final venue on numerous occasions. On December 16th 1950, it was chosen to host a representative game between the Metropolitan League and Western League, an honour repeated on April 12th 1952. The Manor was also used by the Oxfordshire FA for county games and for important matches featuring Oxford Boys' teams. The first international game to take place in Headington was on March 30th 1968, when 3,300 spectators watched England play Wales in a schoolboy fixture. On March 25th 1972, Yeovil Town and Stafford met at the Manor in the semi-final of the FA Trophy, with 6,566 watching Stafford win 4-0. On October 10th 1972, only 1,500 spectators turned up to watch Stoke City play Wolves in Arthur Turner's testimonial. On March 6th 1976, England's under-15s met Northern Ireland, and on February 6th 1991, England played Denmark in an under-19 international that ended goalless. On February 28th 1993, with United away at Barnsley, the ground played host to the Women's FA Cup final in which Arsenal beat Doncaster Belles 3-0. The ground was also the venue for a first-round FA Cup second replay between Oxford City and Wycombe Wanderers on November 16th 1999, which the Chairboys won 1-0.

INTERNATIONAL VENUE

ON July 8th 2002 the Kassam Stadium hosted the Uefa under-17 championship, featuring England, Italy, Brazil, and the Czech Republic. The second round was at Birmingham's St. Andrew's, with the final back at the Kassam on July 14th. The first game, between Brazil and the Czechs, ended 1-1 with Evandro opening the scoring for Brazil with a retaken penalty, with Vlastimil Fiala netting a late equaliser. In the second game, England were twice in front through goals from Luke Moore, but Italy came back with strikes from Piermarino Morosini and Alessandro Simonetta. The attendance was 5,292. For the final between England and Brazil there was a crowd of over 10,000. James Milner scored in the eighth minute, with Jailson equalising on the hour. In stoppage time Brazil had Junior sent off for a scything tackle on Aaron Lennon and the game ended 1-1. The draw was sufficient to give England overall victory in the competition. On May 19th 2009, the Kassam hosted the final of the International Challenge Trophy between England C and Belgium under-21s. England, featuring Oxford striker James Constable, lost 1-0 to a goal from Club Brugge's Brecht Capon.

CONCERT HALL

THE Kassam has also hosted a large-scale outdoor concert. On June 24th 2006, around 16,500 people attended an Elton John show where he played a set-list comprising 22 songs, beginning with Bennie And The Jets and concluding with Your Song. The Manor was also a venue for rock concerts, with three bands playing on a stage set up on the Beech Road terrace before games in the 1974/75 season. First to play were Ace, who performed before United played Fulham on October 26th, followed by Starry Eyed & Laughing, who appeared on December 7th before United played Hull City. Brinsley Schwarz were the final band to play, before United's match against Cardiff City on December 14th. However, complaints about the noise from neighbouring households forced the innovation to be abandoned. During the mid-1990s, the Oxford United Supporters' Club was set up as a venue under the name of The Kooler and several local bands played there, including the Candyskins, Catatonia, and Arthur Turner's Lovechild? among others. ATL? even signed their first record deal, with Rotator, on the Manor pitch on August 5th 1995, just before Oxford beat West Ham 3-2 in the Oxfordshire Benevolent Cup final.

THE GAME OF HIS LIFE

THERE are not many World Cup captains who have appeared for United – still less one who captained his team to one of the greatest World Cup upsets recorded – but Ed McIlvenny can claim that proud record. Born on October 21st 1924 in Greenock, Scotland, McIlvenny's first clubs were Klondyke Athletic Juniors and his school side, St. Mungo's RC School. He was selected for a Scottish Junior League side before joining Wrexham, at the age of 22. He played seven games for them until, in 1949, he moved to the United States to stay with his sister in New York. While there, he joined Philadelphia Nationals in the American Soccer League and his performances for them earned him a call-up to the US national side for the 1950 World Cup in Brazil. Playing at right-half, he played all three games and was chosen as captain for the game against England in Belo Horizonte. The United States shocked the world by beating England 1-0, with a goal from Joe Gaetjens. After the World Cup, McIlvenny joined Manchester United, having impressed Matt Busby with a display against them for a Kearny-Philadelphia All-Star team. He played twice for the Red Devils before joining Waterford in the Republic of Ireland. He played for the League of Ireland representative team against the Irish League in Dublin, the Hessen League of Germany in Frankfurt, and the Hessen League in Kassel. In 1957 he joined Headington United, playing 39 games for the U's. He retired in November 1958 and moved to Eastbourne to run a football school. McIlvenny died in Eastbourne on May 18th 1989.

DÍAZ OF OUR LIVES

AS well as a World Cup captain, United can boast a World Cup winner, albeit the under-20s version. United manager Ramon Díaz played for Argentina in the 1979 Tokyo Under-20 World Cup, scoring a hat-trick in the first game as Indonesia were demolished 5-0; Diego Maradona netted the other two goals. Díaz also scored a hat-trick in Argentina's 5-0 quarter-final win over Algeria, and scored the first in the 2-0 semi-final victory against Uruguay. Argentina beat the Soviet Union 3-1 in the final, with Díaz again on the scoresheet. Díaz then played four times for Argentina in the 1982 World Cup in Spain, scoring in Argentina's final game, a 3-1 defeat by Brazil.

THE WORLD IN MOTION

ED McIlvenny isn't the only United player to have played in a World Cup finals. Dorchester-born Mark Wright featured six times for England in the 1990 tournament in Italy, during which he scored the only goal of the game against Egypt as England eventually reached the semi-finals. Wright won 44 England caps and is the only product of United's youth team to become a full England international. Billy Hamilton won 41 caps for Northern Ireland, including five at the Spain World Cup in 1982. Hamilton famously crossed the ball for Gerry Armstrong to score the winner against Spain in Valencia, and then scored both goals in the next game as Northern Ireland drew with Austria in Madrid. He won a further three caps in Mexico four years later when he was with Oxford, making him the only player to have appeared in a World Cup finals while on United's books. Both Ray Houghton and John Aldridge appeared for the Republic of Ireland in the 1990 World Cup finals in Italy and the 1994 finals in the USA. Both players played in all five of the Republic's games in Italy, with Houghton scoring one of the penalties in the shoot-out that saw Ireland beat Romania to qualify for the quarter-finals. Houghton also scored the goal that gave Ireland a 1-0 win over Italy in New York in 1994, while Aldridge scored in the 2-1 defeat to Mexico in Orlando. Houghton won four caps in the USA, but Aldridge missed the final game, a 2-0 defeat to the Netherlands. Steve Foster won one of his three England caps playing in a 1-0 win over Kuwait in Spain in 1982. Goalkeeper Andre Arendse represented South Africa in three games in South Korea at the 2002 World Cup finals, keeping one clean sheet in a 1-0 win over Slovenia. Another goalkeeper, Ian Walker, who played three games for United when on loan from Spurs in 1990, appeared three times for England in the 1991 Under-20 World Cup in Portugal. He kept one clean sheet, in a goalless draw against Uruguay. Mark Stein, despite being born in Cape Town, South Africa, featured twice for England in the 1985 Under-20 World Cup in Azerbaijan. Irish defender Barry Quinn played four times for the Republic in the 1999 Under-20 World Cup in Nigeria. And, although never an Oxford player, United manager Graham Rix played five times for England in the 1982 finals in Spain.

C YOU LATER

UNITED have had six players called up to represent England C, the international side for non-league players. First was winger Andy Burgess, who scored on his debut against Scotland in a 3-0 win on May 25th 2007. He also played against Wales two days later in the same Four Nations tournament. Matt Day and Luke Foster both played for England C in the 6-2 defeat by Bosnia & Herzegovina on September 16th 2008, with Day scoring one of England's consolation goals. James Constable scored on his England C debut in a 2-2 draw in Italy on November 12th 2008 in the International Challenge Trophy. He also played for England in the final of that tournament, played at the Kassam Stadium on May 19th 2009, but England were beaten 1-0 by Belgium. Matt Green played in a 1-1 draw in Hungary on September 15th 2009, while the most recent England C player is Sam Deering, who played in a 2-1 win over Ireland on May 19th 2010. One of the club's earliest known international players was Henry James Potts, who played three times for Headington as an amateur in 1950. Potts was also an Oxford University player, and was registered for Pegasus FC, the combined Oxford and Cambridge universities team. On April 8th 1950, Potts won one of his eight England Amateur international caps, and was England's best player, in a 0-0 draw with France.

TREE FELLERS

THE most Oxford players to play together in the same national side is three, when David Langan, Ray Houghton, and John Aldridge featured for the Republic of Ireland on March 26th 1986 in a 1-0 defeat by Wales. Playing for Wales that day was United forward Jeremy Charles, which makes this game the international featuring most Oxford players and also the only occasion that Oxford players have featured on opposite sides in an international fixture. The Irish triumvirate also played together in Ireland's 1-1 draw with Uruguay on April 23rd 1986 and in a 2-2 draw with Belgium on September 10th in the European Championships qualifiers. In the same tournament the trio featured in a 0-0 draw with Scotland on October 15th and a 1-0 defeat by Poland on November 12th 1986. After Aldridge's sale to Liverpool, Houghton and Langan played together twice more for Ireland while both on Oxford's books, in 2-0 and 2-1 wins over Luxembourg in May and September 1987.

IN THE NET

SINCE United turned professional, 12 players have scored 50 or more goals in their Oxford careers. Steve Basham just missed out, with 49 goals, but Paul Simpson scored one more to make it into this prestigious list. Geoff Denial scored one more than Simmo, while Joey Beauchamp was the highest-scoring midfielder with 77 goals. Peter Foley and John Aldridge each scored 90 goals for United, although Aldo did it in fewer than half of Foley's appearances, Aldridge playing 141 games for the U's, against Foley's 321. Tony Jones scored exactly a century of goals in his 356 games, with 53 goals coming in 103 appearances before United joined the League. United's leading goalscorer is Graham Atkinson, who scored 107 goals in 398 games between September 1959 and April 1974. Atkinson is also United's leading Football League scorer, with 77 goals to Aldridge's 72 and Foley's 71. United's top Southern League scorers were Bud Houghton and Wales international Billy Rees, who both scored 52 goals. Oxford's leading goalscorer in the Conference is James Constable, with 52 goals, despite having a hat-trick discounted after Chester's results were expunged.

NOT IN THE NET

TEN players (excluding goalkeepers) have played over 50 games for the U's without finding the net. Wayne Hatswell made 52 appearances without scoring and Andy Kingston had 57 goalless games. Ray Train played 61 games and Malcolm McIntosh 67 with no joy in front of goal. Canadian international Mark Watson had 68 games without scoring while John Lloyd played 74 matches and John Doyle 80, also without scoring. Future FA secretary Ted Croker failed to score in his 91 games for Headington United, while long-standing right-back Gary Smart played an incredible 204 games with no goals to his name. There was even a Gary Smart Society, which made a substantial amount of money by gambling on Smart's non-scoring record. Smart's non-achievement pales into insignificance compared to that of Pat Quartermain. The Oxford-born full-back made his debut on September 24th 1955 and by the time he played his final game, on March 27th 1967, he had made 305 appearances, during which he had failed to score. However, in his single season at Cambridge United, Quartermain broke his duck in September 1967, scoring in a 4-1 win over Guildford City, in which Bud Houghton also scored twice.

A QUESTION OF DEGREE

JACK Cross wasn't the only Oxford player to have a degree, as you'd expect from a club based in the city with the oldest university in the English-speaking world. United's most well-known alumnus is New Zealand international Ceri Evans, who played for United while studying as a Rhodes Scholar in 1989. While on United's books Evans earned a first-class honours degree in experimental psychology at Worcester College. He also played for the University in the Varsity match against Cambridge at Highbury, scoring in a 3-2 win. Phil Whelan played for United at the same time as Evans, having earned a degree in accountancy at the University of East Anglia. Latvian international striker Kristaps Grebis also possessed a degree, while England amateur international Henry Potts studied at Keble and played for Oxford university and Pegasus. Potts also played in three Varsity fixtures, scoring in the 5-4 win over Cambridge in 1948/49 – the highest-scoring Varsity match – and captaining Oxford in the following season's 2-2 draw at White Hart Lane. After leaving Oxford, French full-back Christophe Remy earned a masters degree in sports management at the Audencia Nantes School of Management and also a masters degree in e-business at the ESCP-EAP European School of Management. Ben Purkiss earned a law degree and represented Great Britain in the 2009 World Student games in Belgrade.

TAXI!

TREVOR Aylott joined Oxford from Birmingham City in 1991. Although he was only at the Manor for one season, he made a big impact with his headband and his famous two-handed 'Aylott wave'. He scored six goals in his 40 games. After leaving Oxford he joined Gillingham, but after just ten appearances left for Bromley. After coaching at Millwall's academy, Aylott took the 'Knowledge' and became a London cabbie. Another United player who took up driving taxis was goalkeeper Jimmy Glass, who famously scored for Carlisle in the last minute of their game against Plymouth to keep the Cumbrians in the Football League at Scarborough's expense. He joined Oxford from Brentford, but played just twice for United before dropping out of the league to play for Crawley Town. He now runs a taxi business in Wimborne Minster, Dorset. In his biography, *One Hit Wonder*, written by Roger Lytollis, Glass expounds upon his career, including his frustrating time at Oxford, and his gambling addiction.

ATOMIC

UNITED striker Jack Cross, Headington's top scorer in his only season at the Manor, was also a worker at the Atomic Energy Research Establishment. Born in Bury, he joined Blackpool as an amateur in 1944. He made his debut aged 17, replacing Stanley Matthews, who was on England duty. After completing his National Service, Cross signed for Bournemouth and while there he earned a degree in economics. In 1953 Bournemouth rejected a bid for him from Blackpool, then one of the biggest clubs in the country, and he demanded a transfer. Bournemouth sold Cross to Northampton for a record fee of £6,000. He scored 26 goals in 54 games before breaking his ankle against Wolves. As a result of his injury he applied for a job as a higher executive officer at the Atomic Energy Authority at Harwell, necessitating a transfer to Reading, who paid £6,000 for him. Cross scored seven goals in 16 games before joining Headington United in February 1957. Ongoing injuries prevented him from making his debut until August 24th, against Cheltenham Town; four days later he scored a hat-trick against Tonbridge. Cross played 40 games for United and scored 27 goals, until his work took him to Winfrith and he joined Weymouth. Cross died in 2006, aged 78.

THE FIRST VOICE YOU WILL HEAR IS...

A HEADINGTON United player who earned greater fame was Ted Croker. He joined the club in 1953 after leaving the RAF, having previously played for Charlton Athletic. He played 91 games for the U's, without scoring, but in April 1955, as Headington beat Oxford City in the Smith Memorial Cup, Croker fell awkwardly and broke his leg. Although Croker wasn't insured, the club was and they gave him the £500 they claimed. When he regained fitness, Croker became a youth coach at Cheltenham Town while setting up in business. In September 1973, Croker replaced Denis Follows as general secretary of the Football Association, one of the highest-profile jobs in British football. Croker was responsible for shaping the FA's policy in the wake of the Bradford fire and the Heysel riots, and was on the committee which appointed (and sacked) England managers. It was his idea that the Charity Shield should be played at Wembley between the league champions and the FA Cup winners. Croker died on Christmas Day 1992, aged 68.

A FAIR COP

A NUMBER of United players went on to forge a career on the thin blue line. Jack Capper played 11 games for Headington in 1955 but retired injured, aged 29, in 1961, while at Lincoln City. He joined the Lincolnshire Police and was promoted to detective sergeant in 1971. After retiring he returned to Wales where he died in March 2009. Neil Slatter was a Wales defender whose career was ended through injury in 1991. He retired to Cardiff while joining Gloucester City to play part-time and pound the beat, but he managed just 52 minutes for the Tigers before he was substituted and he never played for the club again. Former postman Keith Cassells left Oxford to join Southampton, at the same time as Mark Wright, for a then record £115,000 each. He played for Brentford and Mansfield Town before becoming a policeman. Gary Watson came up through the Oxford youth ranks before leaving for Carlisle United, with Hughie McGrogan, in a joint deal for £19,000 in May 1980. He also joined the police force after finishing playing, as did Davy Jones, Oxford's first black player, who left for Torquay United in 1972 after just 24 first-team appearances in three seasons, while home-grown defender Nick Lowe became a policeman in Australia after leaving Halifax and joining Mooroolbark. Kevin Francis was signed from Birmingham City in 1998. At 6ft 7ins, Francis was possibly the tallest player to play for United, and in his two years at the club he endeared himself to supporters, earning the nickname 'Bambi on Ice', and joined the London Road end to lead the cheering. He returned to Stockport in 2000 and had spells at Exeter City and Hull City before dropping out of the league. After playing for Studley in 2005, Francis moved to Calgary in Alberta, Canada to become a police officer. More recently, left-back Matt Robinson became a bobby. Robbo played 192 games for the U's after joining from Reading in 2002, eventually joining Forest Green Rovers and then Salisbury City. He went part-time when he became a policeman, having most recently played for Swindon Supermarine. Alan Willey took a slightly different path after his football career ended. Willey was signed by Oxford from Bridgwater Town in 1961 after impressing during an FA Cup tie against United. After 128 games he left for Millwall, finishing his career at Banbury United, where he arrived via Durban City in South Africa. After hanging up his boots, Willey became a prison warden.

A YEAR TO REMEMBER

WHEN Oxford won the Division Three championship in 1983/84, they broke a number of records. Their 95 points was four more than the previous highest Third Division total, set the preceding season by Portsmouth. United became the first side from Division Three to reach the fifth rounds of both the FA Cup and the League Cup in the same season, and the 18 games that they played to get that far was a record for any side from outside the top flight. In December 1983, Kevin Brock became the first player from the Third Division to be voted Young Player of the Month, and his three caps for England under-21 was the most for an outfield player from Division Three: Brock played in a 3-1 win over Italy in the Uefa Championship semi-final first leg, was on the bench for the second leg, and played in both legs of the final against Spain, with England winning 1-0 in Seville and 2-0 at Bramall Lane to win 3-0 on aggregate. Brock was also one of four United players selected for the Third Division PFA Team of the Season, along with Trevor Hebberd, Bobby McDonald, and Malcolm Shotton, which equalled the divisional record. In addition, Steve Biggins' 24 goals beat Colin Booth's previous Oxford league record of 23 goals, set in 1964/65. United also scored more goals (118) than in any season since joining the Football League, and had fewer defeats (seven), and more wins (36) than in their previous league history.

FIXED BY JIM

IN the 1984/85 season, United's cup exploits continued, including a superlative 3-2 win over First Division leaders Arsenal. United's goalscorers were John Aldridge, Billy Hamilton, and David Langan with a 30-yard screamer that Pat Jennings could only palm into his net. However, this result so irked Stephen Gray, a 10-year-old Arsenal supporter, that he wrote to Jimmy Savile to complain. As a consequence, Stephen was permitted to take charge of a rematch between the sides at the Manor, for the BBC programme *Jim'll Fix It*, aired on Saturday 9th February 1985. During the game Stephen sent off the whole Oxford team to allow Arsenal to win the rematch, although in real life it was still United who went through to the fourth round, where they lost 2-1 at Ipswich.

CARIBBEAN

TWO Oxford players have been called up to represent national sides from the Caribbean; Kevin Francis won two caps for St. Kitts & Nevis, despite being born in Moseley – he played in a 2-1 defeat by Dominica, and a 2-1 victory over Guadeloupe in the 1998 Shell Caribbean Cup, but failed to score. Steve Anthrobus (born in Lewisham) was selected to play for Barbados in their World Cup qualifiers against Costa Rica and Guatemala in July 2000, but he couldn't be registered as a Barbadan citizen in time so had to fly home. However, Joe Cooke, United's only native Caribbean, born in Dominica, was never chosen to represent his country. Jefferson Louis, born in Harrow, was capped by Dominica against Barbados in March 2008, while with Mansfield Town.

INTERNATIONAL

UNITED have occasionally faced national opposition. On March 22nd 1954, the FA sent an England amateur international trial team before they played against Scotland at Wembley. This had always been an honour reserved for Football League clubs, but a Manor crowd of 8,000 saw United justify the FA's decision with a 3-0 win, with two goals from Cyril Toulouse and one from Don Crombie. South Africa visited the Manor for the first game of their UK tour on September 17th 1958. Two goals from Johnny Love, one a penalty, earned United a 2-2 draw. On January 29th 1968, a Graham Atkinson goal gave United a 1-0 win over a British Olympic XI, while another British Olympic side beat the U's 1-0 on November 9th 1970. On February 6th 1979, United beat the Denmark under-21 side 2-0 with goals from Paul Berry and a David Fogg penalty. On May 15th 1985, the U's were beaten 5-0 by Bulgaria in Sofia after a goalless first half, in front of 30,000 spectators. This was a World Cup warm-up game for Bulgaria, who beat Yugoslavia 2-1 a fortnight later to qualify for Mexico. In January 1987 United entered the Bermuda Invitational Tournament, beating the Bermuda National XI 5-2 with goals from Billy Whitehurst, Ray Houghton, David Leworthy, Brian McDermott, and John Trewick. In March 1987, Oxford played a Northern Ireland XI in a testimonial for Billy Hamilton, who had played just 41 games in two years at Oxford. United won 6-4, with Hamilton bagging a hat-trick plus goals from David Langan, Les Phillips, and Kevin Brock.

MUSICAL BISCUIT

UNITED have had several songs devoted to them over the years. The first known piece was Upstreet's single United Are Back (In Division Two), released to celebrate promotion in 1984. The track featured the memorable line; "Bobby Robson should play the whole darned lot, except Bobby McDonald for he's a Scot." Upstreet followed this up the following year with We Are The Oxford to commemorate promotion to the First Division. In April 1986, the club released their official Milk Cup final song Oxford United My Oh My, with backing music by Prism and vocals by Trina King, while Kidlington band Tekneek 6 recorded It's A Wembley Final Now. The next offering appeared in February 1989 when the United fanzine *Raging Bull* gave away free copies of a flexi disc by Maxwell House entitled Kevin! in honour of chairman Kevin Maxwell. In 1995 the Oxford United squad recorded U Are My Sunshine with Arthur Turner's Lovechild? (the only band to be named after an Oxford manager) and Sam from Beaker. The next song about United was recorded in 2004 by an ad hoc band called Yellow Army, featuring members of the Rock Of Travolta, Chamfer, Mr Duck, and the Mon£yshots. The track Proud To Be An Oxford Fan was supposed to be given away with the *Rage On* fanzine (the successor to *Raging Bull*) but instead was made available as a download on the Rage Online website (along with the Kevin! flexi). More recently, an artist called U-Man released a track called You Are My Oxford to celebrate Oxford's play-off appearance against Exeter City in 2007. For United's 2010 play-off final appearance U-Man produced Yellow Ribbon. Both songs are available as downloads on MySpace.

SONGS OF REMEMBRANCE

AS well as songs about Oxford, over the years other tracks have become associated with the club. The tannoy at the Manor used to blast out Pilot's Magic whenever United won. Banbury-born Paul Gadd, better known as Gary Glitter, had his I'm The Leader Of The Gang (I Am) become United's entry music. Other songs that have welcomed the U's onto the pitch include the theme tune to children's TV programme *Banana Splits*, Coldplay's Yellow, and Thin Lizzy's The Boys Are Back In Town.

CRAZY EIGHTS

THREE players have scored eight goals in a game in United's history. Harold Knowles did it in a friendly against Cygnets Seconds on October 16th 1897, as Headington FC won 11-0, with Grimsley and B Edney scoring two of the other goals. Percy Drewitt scored eight when Headington United beat Banbury Harriers 9-0 in the Oxfordshire Senior League on December 24th 1921. Left-back Jimmy Ing scored the other goal. Drewitt's feat is all the more remarkable for the fact that he scored all his goals in succession, setting a new local record for consecutive goalscoring. The other eight-ball is Charlie Machin, whose octet occurred when the U's beat Banbury Harriers 16-1 in the Senior League in January 1939.

PARDON THE PUNDIT

THE first ex-United player who turned his hand to the media was former goalkeeper and future New Age conspiracy theorist David Icke. Icke spent three months on loan to Oxford from Coventry City in 1970, although he never played for United's first team. After leaving Hereford United, Icke became a reporter in Leicester, graduating to the television as sports presenter for BBC's *South Today*. He eventually became a presenter on *Grandstand* until 1990, when his involvement with the Green Party as national media spokesperson led him to stand down. It was in 1990 that Icke began forming his 'alternative' ideas following a session with a medium. These eventually became the basis of his reptilian-humanoid theory. Another media personality from United is Ron Atkinson; the former U's captain became a pundit with ITV, a role in which he continued after finishing in football management. His bizarre 'little eyebrows', 'lollipops', and 'early doors' type expressions were known as *Ronglish* and became part of football's lexicon. In April 2004, Atkinson resigned from ITV after he was caught on air uttering a racist remark. Ray Houghton became a pundit after retiring in May 2000. He is seen regularly on Sky and RTE, and also appears on the radio show *Talksport*. Houghton's contemporary John Aldridge is a pundit for the Radio City radio station, where he summarises Liverpool's games, and former Oxford manager Mark Lawrenson appears regularly on BBC's *Match Of The Day*, handing out his expert analysis. Robbie Mustoe, who captained Middlesbrough in the Premiership after leaving Oxford, is now a commentator with ESPN in America.

STRANGERS IN A STRANGE LAND

OXFORD'S first overseas tour was to southern Spain in May 1971 where they beat Lorca CF 1-0 with a Graham Atkinson goal, Atletico Orihuela 2-0 with two Atkinson goals, and CD Almoradi 3-1 with goals from Atkinson, John Evanson, and Derek Clarke. The club had attempted to visit Switzerland the previous May to play Lausanne, but couldn't get the required guarantees. In May 1973, Oxford visited Norway where they played four games, winning them all. They opened with a 3-0 win over Adger Kretslag, followed by beating Sandefjord 7-1 and then Grue 4-1, when Hugh Curran scored a hat-trick. The final game of the tour was a 3-2 win over Stromgodset, who lost by a record 11-0 to Liverpool in the following year's European Cup Winners' Cup. In May 1975, Oxford visited Tunisia for the Sahara Beach Soccer Tournament, where they beat Gillingham 4-2 before losing 3-1 to Peterborough United in the final. The U's played two games in Ireland in August 1983, drawing 2-2 with Shamrock Rovers and beating Sligo Rovers 4-0. In May 1986, United visited Bulgaria, where they lost 5-0 to the national team, followed by a game against Septemvriisk Slava, which Oxford won 2-1 despite some allegedly appallingly biased refereeing. Two months later Oxford went back to Bulgaria, losing 1-0 to Constanta of Romania and 3-2 to Bulgaria's Varna Spartak in the Varna Summer Cup. United then visited Ireland where they were beaten 2-1 by Abertillary, and drew 1-1 with Derry City. In January 1987, Oxford visited the Caribbean to play in the Bermuda Invitational Tournament, beating a Bermuda XI 5-2 before losing 1-0 in the final to Swedish side Malmo. In July that year the U's visited Sweden for a five-game tour, with United winning four games; they beat Edsbro 4-0, Skarblacka 9-1, Trosa 11-0, and Hofors 9-1. The other game was a 1-1 draw with Brommapojkarna. On August 7th 1989, Oxford won 2-1 at Limerick City, and the last time that Oxford left these shores was to play in the Isle of Man tournament in July 1990. United reached the final with a 1-1 draw against Blackpool followed by a 7-1 win over the hosts, but they lost 3-1 to Motherwell in the last game. John Durnin was the tournament's leading scorer with six goals. Oxford have also twice visited Guernsey. The first occasion on August 4th 1971, United won 10-0, but the second game, played at Corbett's Field on January 22nd 1979, was a 1-1 draw.

CHUNG-HO!

SAMMY (Cyril) Chung was one of only two British-born oriental footballers to play in the Football League (the other was Frank Soo of Stoke, Luton, and England). He was born in Abingdon to a Chinese father and English mother. He joined Headington United as an amateur in 1950, aged 18, becoming the side's first non-white player, and made his first-team debut on December 17th 1951, in a 2-1 win over Worcester City, having already scored a hat-trick in a 4-2 friendly win over Abingdon Town on November 18th. Chung also played in the first floodlit game, a 3-0 win over Banbury Spencer on December 18th. Chung was a nippy left winger who had previously captained his school team. He made 20 appearances for Headington, scoring 11 goals before his final game, a 4-3 defeat at Exeter City reserves on November 10th 1951. He had been scouted by Reading's manager Ted Drake, who offered him £6 a week to sign professionally. Although Headington matched the offer, the lure of playing in the Football League proved too much for Chung, who left the Manor for Elm Park. Chung went on to play for Norwich City and Watford, and later managed alongside Bill McGarry at Watford, Ipswich Town, and Wolves before taking over from McGarry at Molineux. He went on to manage Vasteras, in Sweden.

I'M A BELIEVER

UNITED'S first black player was David Frederic Jones, who was born in Brixham, Devon. Davy Jones joined Oxford after an unsuccessful trial with Middlesbrough, having previously been on Arsenal's books. He made his Oxford debut on October 9th 1968, in a 1-0 home defeat by Carlisle United, and went on to play 24 times for the U's, four as a substitute. His only goal for the club came in a 2-0 win over Northampton Town in a League Cup first round tie on August 13th 1969. After losing his first-team place to John Shepherd, Jones starred for the reserves as they finished second in the Football Combination in 1971/72, after which he joined Torquay United on a free transfer. He made just one substitute appearance for the Gulls before returning to Oxfordshire to play for Witney Town. After playing for Hungerford he joined Oxford City as player-manager in 1986, having played for them three years previously. He went on to become a police officer.

CAPTAIN COOKE

UNITED'S first black captain was Joe Cooke. Cooke was born in Roseau, on the island of Dominica in the Caribbean, and he joined Bradford City in July 1970, having come to England as a child. In January 1979 he moved to Peterborough United for £45,000, joining Oxford for £50,000 seven months later. Cooke started at Oxford as a striker, scoring on his debut in a 2-2 draw at Hull City on August 25th 1979. However, after losing form he dropped back to partner Gary Briggs in defence, but still finished as top league goalscorer in 1980/81 with six goals. In total, Cooke played 79 games for Oxford, scoring 13 goals, before leaving for Exeter City in 1981.

SECOND-CHOICE BOSS

HARRY Thompson was appointed Headington United's player-coach on August 1st 1949, but the former Wolves and Northampton player wasn't the board's first choice. The club had initially approached former Spurs and Reading player Ronnie Dix for the post, but this information was leaked to the *Berkshire Chronicle* by the man from whom the club had asked for Dix's address. As a result, Dix was approached by four other clubs the following day and his services were lost to Headington. Dix is famous for being the youngest goalscorer in Football League history, scoring for Bristol Rovers aged 15 years 180 days. He also won one England cap, scoring against Norway in a friendly in 1938. Headington had also been negotiating with Spurs' Cyril Trailor, but he went to Leyton Orient instead.

FIRST CONTACT

ALF Jenkins was a Harwell scientist. He was also a midfielder signed from Bury in March 1950, making his debut at Exeter City reserves in a 1-0 defeat. As well as being on the losing side this was an inauspicious debut for Jenkins for another reason, as the short-sighted player wore glasses and he broke them during the game. As a result, Jenkins had a pair of contact lenses fitted, which he wore in his next game at Torquay United reserves, a 2-0 defeat. The lenses cost in the region of £35 and it is likely that Jenkins was the first Headington player to wear them. Jenkins played 44 games for United, scoring twice, before joining Mossley.

WORKING ON THE CHAIN GANG

WHEN Southern League Headington United met First Division Bolton Wanderers in the FA Cup fourth round on January 30th 1954, it was the first time a team from Oxfordshire had met top-flight opposition in a competitive game, and it was the furthest that a local side had gone in the competition. Wins against Third Division (South) Millwall and Third Division (North) Stockport County in the previous rounds – both won 1-0 after replays – were made even more impressive by the fact that many of the Headington players combined playing football with holding down regular jobs, training at the Manor in the evenings under floodlights. Goalkeeper Jack Ansell was a poultry farmer with a smallholding near Bletchley, while full-back Ted Croker ran a garage in Chipping Norton. Centre-half Bobby Craig was a carpenter who worked on building sites, and right-half Ernie Hudson was an electrician. Left-half Johnnie Crichton worked alongside outside-right Ronnie Steel in a fancy goods factory, where they made ladies' slippers. Inside-left Ben Duncan was a painter and decorator, and inside-right Tom McGarrity was a fully qualified physiotherapist, the first and only male to hold that position at the Cowley Road Hospital.

IN THE (WRONG) NET

THE first recorded own goal scored for United was a header by W. Couling in the City Junior League final replay against St. Mary Magdalene on March 16th 1899. Headington won the match 3-0, with Couling's goal coming shortly before the final whistle. Since 1949, Oxford's opponents have scored own goals on United's behalf in 83 games. The first was on November 5th 1949, when Bedford's Potter contributed to a 2-0 win for Headington, and the most recent was against Thurrock in the FA Cup fourth qualifying round on October 24th 2009, when Lee Flynn deflected a Sam Deering cross into his own net. However, on only two occasions has the opposition performed the feat twice in a game; on February 24th 1954, United hosted Gravesend & Northfleet in a Southern League Cup second round tie and won 3-1, with two of Headington's goals coming from Gravesend's left-back Lewis and centre-half Chambers. On Boxing Day 1958, Corby Town were the visitors to the Manor and in an incredible game the Steelmen were beaten 7-3. Included in Headington's seven goals were own goals by Neilson and W. Morris.

AVERAGE BUT DIFFERENT

AT the start of the 1976/77 season, goal difference (goals scored minus goals conceded) replaced goal average (goals scored divided by goals conceded) as a means of separating teams equal on points. When Headington won the Southern League in 1952/53 they had the same number of points (58) as Merthyr Tydfil, but United's goal average was 1.86 compared with the Welsh side's 1.77. If goal difference had been the method of deciding positions, Merthyr would have won the title with a goal difference of +51.

	P	W	D	L	F	A	Pts	Ave
Headington United	**42**	**23**	**12**	**7**	**93**	**50**	**58**	**1.86**
Merthyr Tydfil	42	25	8	9	117	66	58	1.77
Bedford Town	42	24	8	10	91	61	56	1.09

This made up for United's second-place finish in the Oxfordshire Senior League in 1945/46, when they lost the Section A title to Milton RAF on goal average:

	P	W	D	L	F	A	Pts	Ave
Milton RAF	12	9	2	1	45	19	20	2.37
Headington United	**12**	**9**	**2**	**1**	**51**	**22**	**20**	**2.31**
Oxford City Reserves	12	6	2	4	44	28	14	1.57
Benson RAF	12	5	1	6	34	41	11	0.83
GWR Sports	12	2	3	7	22	50	7	0.44
Brize Norton RAF	12	3	0	9	30	31	6	0.97
RNAS Culham	12	2	2	8	26	62	6	0.42

POINTLESS (ALMOST)

HEADINGTON'S most unsuccessful season was undoubtedly 1909/10, when the side finished bottom of the Oxfordshire League Division Two, Section 'A' with just one point from their nine games. They drew 1-1 with Radley on November 6th for their solitary point, and scratched their game at Dorchester on February 19th, which is why an odd number of matches is recorded.

PAYING THE PENALTY

UNITED'S first official appearance in a penalty shoot-out was in the Zenith Data Systems Cup (previously the Full Members Cup) first round, on November 21st 1990. Bristol City were the visitors and the game ended 2-2, with Jim Magilton and Lee Nogan scoring for the U's. The crowd of 1,323 then saw the game go to penalties, with Ronnie Sinclair saving Les Robinson's kick before Mark Aizlewood shot over. Paul Simpson scored his penalty, as did City's Andy May, followed by goals from Nogan and Rob Newman. Sinclair then saved from Joey Beauchamp before Ken Veysey kept out Dave Smith's spot-kick. Magilton put away his penalty before Veysey brilliantly saved from David Rennie to give United a 3-2 victory. United appeared in a penalty shoot-out in the same tournament the following season, this time losing 4-3 on penalties after drawing 3-3 at Swindon Town. Andy Melville and Paul Simpson (2) had scored for Oxford in the game, but David Penney missed the first penalty, and Trevor Aylott then blasted over. Duncan Shearer scored the final spot kick to win the tie.

WAR – WHAT IS IT GOOD FOR?

HEADINGTON United perhaps had more reason than many to rue the outbreak of war. Twice they recorded their best seasons to date, only for their momentum to be disrupted with the declaration of hostilities. In 1913/14 United won the Oxfordshire Junior League Section C for the first time, losing just one of their 12 games, going on to reach the tournament's final where they lost 3-0 to YMCA. They also won the Oxfordshire Junior Shield, beating Oxford Institute 5-2 in the final. However, during the summer, events in Europe led to the start of World War I, and competitive football was suspended for Headington for the next five years, recommencing in 1919. In 1938/39, United were undefeated in 26 Oxfordshire Senior League games, dropping just two points, to win the title, and they won both the Oxford Hospital Cup and the Oxfordshire Charity Cup and reached the final of the Oxfordshire Senior Cup. However, just before the start of the following season England declared war on Germany, throwing preparations into disarray. The season did start, but many clubs had suspended activities and many players had been conscripted, and the league programme was disrupted due to travel restrictions and poor weather.

THE ROAD TO HELL

SINCE the late 1960s, Oxford's main rivals have been neighbours Swindon Town, just 30 miles south-west down the A420 (dubbed the 'Road to Hell' by the *Oxford Mail*, but only because of the large number of traffic accidents along it). The first time the sides met was in Headington United's second match, and Swindon's first, under floodlights at the Manor on January 31st 1951. A crowd of just over 7,000 saw United draw 0-0 with the Division Three (South) side. Swindon visited Headington for another friendly on January 19th 1955, this time winning 2-1 with Harry Yates scoring United's goal. The return match, on February 16th, United's first at the County Ground, was a 1-0 win to Swindon, with Yates missing a penalty for Headington. The crowd was 1,786. United again lost 2-1 in the next friendly, on January 24th 1959, with Jimmy Jackson scoring for Headington. Swindon's next visit to the Manor was for another floodlit friendly, on March 24th 1960, and again United lost 1-0. On May 24th 1963, with United renamed Oxford and playing in the Fourth Division, Swindon visited the Manor for Pat Quartermain's testimonial. John Shuker scored for Oxford, but Swindon, who had just won promotion to Division Two, won 2-1, with 5,374 in attendance. Two years later the sides met as equals in their first competitive fixture, a Division Three game on August 21st 1965. United's first Football League visit to the County Ground was witnessed by 20,409, who saw Oxford gain a point in a goalless draw. United lost the return match 3-0 before a crowd of 16,074, the largest to have watched a league match at the Manor at that time. The following season saw the same scorelines but with the venues reversed, and in 1967/68 the Manor league crowd record was broken again when 17,836 saw the sides draw 0-0 on April 12th. Four days later Oxford scored their first league goal against Swindon, when Graham Atkinson's strike earned a 1-1 draw at the County Ground. With United earning promotion there was a gap of one season before Swindon joined Oxford in Division Two. On September 13th 1969, 21,903 – the largest crowd to have watched the derby – saw a 0-0 draw in Swindon. On May 6th 1970, the sides met in Clanfield for the Clanfield Cup. Oxford won 2-0 with goals from David Sloan and John Evanson, with 1,500 watching. The teams met in the same tournament exactly one year later, Swindon winning on penalties after a 1-1 draw.

ON May 3rd 1972, the sides drew 2-2 in Clanfield, with Brian Thompson and Roy Clayton scoring for Oxford, who won the penalty shoot-out 4-3. United earned their first competitive win over Swindon on September 24th 1972, when David Sloan's goal knocked the holders out of the League Cup. It wasn't until February 24th 1973 that Oxford earned their first, and so far only, competitive win in Swindon, as goals from Dave Roberts, Nigel Cassidy, and Hugh Curran gave the U's a 3-1 win to complete the double over the Moonrakers for the first and only time, Cassidy having scored the only goal at the Manor on December 16th 1972. Swindon played in Rodney Smithson's testimonial on May 2nd 1975, the game finishing 2-2, and on April 3rd 1976 the sides joined forces to play Witney Town in a charity match in aid of the Houseman-Gillham Children's Fund, for the six children orphaned after Peter Houseman's car crash; the combined team won 1-0. On September 27th 1981 the sides' old boys met at Witney Town's Marriotts Close ground for a charity game, with the ex-Oxford players winning 3-2. Oxford failed to win in the next dozen competitive meetings, but thrashed Swindon 5-0, the biggest scoreline in the derby, on April 7th 1982. On August 5th 1987, Swindon visited the Manor for Gary Briggs' testimonial; Malcolm Shotton scored United's goal in a 3-1 defeat, watched by 4,536. It was another ten meetings before Oxford won again, beating Swindon 5-3 on March 7th 1992. Five meetings later, on March 19th 1996, United won 3-0 as they stormed up Division Three to finish second, behind Swindon. In the 2000/01 season, the last in which the teams met in league action, Swindon did the double over United, with Guy Whittingham scoring his only Oxford goal in his only Oxford game as the U's lost 2-1 at the County Ground, while Swindon won the return game 2-0 on March 10th 2001. The last time the sides met competitively, on Sunday 8th December 2002, was in the FA Cup second round, when a Jefferson Louis header took Oxford through to face Arsenal at Highbury. On December 5th 2003 the sides met in a behind-closed-doors friendly, which Swindon won 1-0, but United were avenged on July 8th 2005, when they visited Swindon for another behind-closed-doors game, this time winning 3-0 with goals from Lee Bradbury, Craig Davies, and trialist Stuart Beavon. In 53 competitive meetings, Oxford have won just ten games, losing 24 times, and scoring 55 goals to Swindon's 80.

FOOLS MATE

IN February 1993, Oxford United played a different kind of match. At the London Simpson's Sim tournament, the U's challenged chess grandmaster Garry Kasparov to a game of chess. Kasparov was White and began with the Bishop's Opening against Oxford's Berlin Defence. Gary Smart was United's main protagonist, but he had no answer to Kasparov's genius and the U's found themselves check mated after 26 moves.

RECORD SCRATCHED

UNITED'S record score is one that, unfortunately, doesn't appear in the record books. On September 22nd 1945, Headington beat Didcot 17-1 at the Manor, with goals from Parker (6), Green (4), 15-year-old Wilson (2), Gordon (2), Machin, a Fletcher own goal, and one unrecorded. The Didcot side included a number of former prisoners of war who were still recuperating after their experiences, and their inferior fitness was possibly a factor in the game's one-sidedness. Didcot resigned from the Oxfordshire Senior League a couple of weeks later, and so their results were expunged from the record books. Later that season, Headington beat the Royal Naval Air Station Culham 13-0 as they finished second in the table, behind Milton RAF on goal average. This means that the side's best recorded score is 16-1 over Banbury Harriers in the Oxfordshire Senior League on January 21st 1939. Charlie Machin scored eight goals, Jack Ramsden a hat-trick, Wally Imms two, goalkeeper Geoff Wyatt one from the penalty spot, and Maurice Lonie and Bert Nutt one apiece. Since turning pro, United have yet to hit double figures in a competitive game, but have scored nine on three occasions.

CONNECTIONS

THERE are more Oxford player connections with Oxford City than any other club, with 42 players having made first-team appearances for both sides, although that number doesn't include the many who went on to join the Hoops without playing for United's first team. Second are Northampton Town, who have had 40 players in common; among the more notable are Les Phillips, Jack Ansell, Martin Aldridge, and Harry Thompson. United and Reading have 38 players in common, including Alan Judge, Les Taylor, Ray Houghton, and Paul Moody. Cardiff City are fourth in the connections game, with 33 players in common, followed by QPR with 32.

CONSORTING WITH THE ENEMY

DESPITE their intense rivalry, 28 players have turned out for both United and Swindon. The earliest was John Thomas, who joined Swindon from Everton, and thence to Headington for whom he played five games at the start of the 1952/53 season, before moving to Chester. Thomas was followed by Bob Peart, who left Swindon for Yeovil Town before arriving at Headington in March 1953. He scored 15 goals in 38 games for the U's but was released in May 1954, later signing for Cheltenham Town. Scottish winger Jimmy Bain joined Headington in July 1954 after seven seasons at the County Ground. He scored seven goals in 80 games over two seasons for United before retiring. Corporal John Skull arrived on loan to Headington from Wolves in February 1955. He started his career as an amateur with Wellington Town before signing for his hometown club, Swindon. A qualified physiotherapist, Skull was a corporal with the Royal Army Medical Corps, stationed at Wheatley Military Hospital, and played for the U's by arrangement with Wanderers. He played 33 games over the next year, scoring 14 goals. Other players who played for both Swindon and Headington were Dave Gibson who joined the Robins from Everton in November 1954. He moved to the Manor in the summer of 1957, playing 97 games and scoring 31 goals over three seasons for United; Alan Gibbs, who came from Swindon after leaving Cardiff, arrived at the same time as Gibson but lasted just three months, playing eight games, before moving to Cheltenham. Gordon Pembery also joined United from Swindon in the summer of 1957, playing 18 games over the course of the season before returning to his native Wales to play for Merthyr Tydfil. Gordon McDonald also moved up the A420 – in 1958 – and he played 30 games for Headington over the next two seasons. Jimmy Cross, another former Everton player, arrived from Swindon at the same time as McDonald and played 32 games in his one season at the Manor. Goalkeeper Owen Medlock joined United from Swindon in December 1959 and was with the U's as they gained election to the Football League. His 133 games included United's first Football League fixture, at Barrow, in August 1962. Another goalkeeping connection is Jim Barron, whom Oxford signed from Chelsea in 1966 before selling him on to Nottingham Forest for £30,000 four years – and 165 appearances – later. Barron joined Swindon from Forest in August 1974.

JOHN Lloyd moved to Oxford from Swindon, for whom he never played, in April 1966. He played 74 games over the course of four seasons before moving to Aldershot. Alan Fursdon arrived at the Manor from Swindon in May 1967, having failed to play for the Wiltshire side. He was with Oxford for over a year, but only played twice, one of those as a substitute, and then joined Dover. Centre-forward Ken Skeen joined United from Swindon in July 1967, going on to play 270 games for Oxford in the next seven years, scoring 40 goals. Irish international goalkeeper Mick Kearns came up through the Oxford youth ranks, making his debut on March 27th 1970 against Leicester City. In May 1970 he joined Swindon on loan to act as an understudy to Peter Downsborough in the Anglo-Italian Cup competition, but didn't get to play. On September 11th 1986, Oxford loaned Mark Jones to Swindon, who five weeks later paid United £30,000 for his permanent services. Berinsfield-born Jones had played 158 games for the U's, scoring seven goals, making his debut as a substitute against Exeter on March 29th 1980. Goalkeeper Kevin Deardon played for Swindon in March 1990 on loan from Spurs. He was at Oxford earlier in the season, but didn't play. Possibly the most well-known connection between Oxford and Swindon is Joey Beauchamp. Coming up through the youth ranks, Beauchamp made his Oxford debut on May 13th 1989 as a substitute against Watford. He made 129 appearances, scoring 22 goals, before a £1 million move to West Ham United. He was there for just 58 days, and didn't play a competitive game for them, before Swindon bought him for a club record £800,000, including defender Adrian Whitbread. He played 56 games in his first season at the County Ground, scoring three goals but, after Steve McMahon replaced John Gorman as manager, Beauchamp fell out of favour and the following season he played just four games, scoring once. In November 1995 Oxford bought Beauchamp for just £75,000, 16 months after selling him. Swindon's Peter Holcroft had a two-week trial at Oxford in February 1998, but United didn't sign him. Marcus Phillips made one substitute appearance for his first club, Swindon Town, from where he joined Cheltenham. He joined Oxford from Witney Town in 1997, making just one substitute appearance, a 1-0 defeat at Huddersfield Town, before emigrating to Australia.

PERIPATETIC goalkeeper Jimmy Glass joined Swindon from AFC Bournemouth in June 1998, and it was while on loan to Carlisle from the Robins that he scored his famous goal to keep the Cumbrians in the Football League. After spells at Cambridge United and Brentford, Glass came to Oxford as reserve to Richard Knight, the keeper he'd replaced at Carlisle. Glass's debut for Oxford was the final league game of his career, a 4-0 defeat at Stoke City, and he also played in a 4-1 LDV Vans Trophy defeat at Brentford before moving to Crawley Town and then Kingstonian. Another goalkeeper, Alan Judge, joined Oxford from Reading in 1984/85 as Steve Hardwick's deputy, displacing him the following season. Judge left Oxford for Hereford United in 1991 after playing 100 games for the club, including the Milk Cup final. He joined Swindon in December 2002, but didn't feature. He returned to Oxford as goalkeeping coach and made two further appearances, in each becoming the club's oldest-ever player. Dominic Foley was a Watford player when he appeared on loan for both Swindon, in January 2002, and Oxford (for whom he played six games), in March 2003. Adrian Viveash started his career at Swindon, debuting in 1990, but it was from Reading where he joined Oxford on loan in September 2002 – playing 15 games for United – after which he returned to Swindon. Tommy Mooney joined Swindon from Birmingham City in July 2003, finishing second-top scorer with 20 goals in his only season at the club. Mooney joined Oxford in July 2004 and played 45 games that season, finishing top scorer with 15 goals, before moving on to Wycombe. Eric Sabin joined Swindon in June 2001 from French side Wasquehal. After two years he moved to QPR, joining Oxford from Northampton Town in August 2005. He played 35 games, scoring nine goals, before returning to France. Patrick Collins played two games for Oxford in November 2007, on loan from Darlington, having played 13 games for Swindon in 2005, on loan from Sheffield Wednesday. Paul Evans played 13 games for Swindon in 2006. He joined Oxford in September 2008, making just four appearances before being released. Alex Rhodes made four substitute appearances for Swindon while on loan from Brentford in October 2006. He joined Oxford from Rotherham United in May 2009, but was released in November after making just three substitute appearances.

BEHIND ENEMY LINES

THERE are links between Oxford and Swindon at management level. Fred Ford became Swindon's manager in July 1969, moving from Bristol Rovers. Under Ford's guidance they won the Anglo-Italian League Cup in 1969 and the Anglo-Italian Cup in 1970. After Ford's dismissal on November 1st 1971 Swindon's next game was a 1-1 draw at Oxford and in his matchday programme notes Oxford's manager Gerry Summers reflected that Ford was: "a person who the game can ill afford to lose." In the summer of 1972 Oxford made Ford their chief scout and youth administrator. Former England international Colin Todd joined Oxford from Nottingham Forest in February 1984, playing 12 games for United as they won the Third Division. After leaving Oxford, Todd played for Vancouver Whitecaps and Luton before dropping out of the Football League. He replaced Jimmy Quinn as Swindon manager in May 2000, but after 18 games in charge he left for Derby County the following October, to be groomed as a successor to Jim Smith. Malcolm Crosby was made Oxford's assistant manager by Denis Smith in September 1973. After Smith's resignation in December 1997, Crosby took charge for a 1-0 defeat at Wolves on Boxing Day. After five games without a win, Crosby joined Smith at West Bromwich Albion. On May 5th 2000, Colin Todd took Crosby to Swindon to be his assistant, and Crosby survived both Todd's departure and his successors, Andy King and Roy Evans, before leaving in the summer of 2004.

SIX OF THE BEST

OXFORD United had six players named in the PFA's 1984/85 Second Division Team of the Season: John Aldridge, Gary Briggs, Billy Hamilton, Trevor Hebberd, Dave Langan, and Malcolm Shotton.

SQUADDIES

TWO recent players have military connections. Guernsey keeper Chris Tardif was accepted for the Royal Military Academy in Sandhurst before a successful trial with Portsmouth caused a career change. Lee Bradbury served in Omagh, Northern Ireland with the Princess of Wales Royal Regiment from 1993 to 1995, before Portsmouth offered him a trial after he impressed against them.

THEY CAME IN PEACE

UNITED'S first recorded game against overseas opposition was on April 23rd 1948, against Dutch side UVS Leyden. The game was played at the Iffley Road ground normally used by Pegasus and Oxford University and was watched by 1,500 people. On May 14th 1951, Royal Ixelles visited from Belgium as part of the Festival of Britain celebrations, and a Manor crowd of 10,000 saw Jim Smith score for Headington in a 1-1 draw. French side US Dunkerquoise visited the Manor on March 7th 1955 and were soundly beaten 8-0 by a rampant Headington, with goals from John Skull (2), Harry Yates, Charles Nicklas, Gordon Johnstone, Johnnie Crichton, Percy Mumford, and an own goal. Four weeks later Headington hosted IFK Stockholm and won 5-1, thanks to two goals from Crichton, two from Nicklas, and one from Ben Duncan. After a 2-2 draw against South Africa in September 1959, United hosted Spandauer Sport Verein, from Germany, on April 9th 1964. Bud Houghton, Arthur Longbottom, and Bill Calder were on target in a 3-1 win, watched by 3,968. Finnish side Valkeakosken Haka visited on April 20th 1966, and were beaten 6-1, thanks to goals by Graham Atkinson (2), Tony Buck (2), Tony Jones, and Peter Morris, before a crowd of 1,982. The next foreign visitors were Ghanaian champions Asante Kotoko on August 4th 1969. Goals from Colin Clarke and John Shuker earned Oxford a 2-0 win, with 4,391 in attendance. Bohemians of Prague were the next European team to brave the Manor, with 3,515 watching a 1-1 draw, with Derek Clarke scoring for United. Oxford were due to have played Shakhtar Donetsk on November 22nd 1971, but because of problems in the Soviet Union the Ukrainians were unable to travel. On October 2nd 1974, SC Bonn lost 3-1 thanks to goals from John Sims (2) and Andy Bodell, before just 926 spectators. On August 9th that year Royal Antwerp became the first foreign opposition to win on Oxford soil, beating United 2-1 in a pre-season friendly. Billy Jeffrey scored United's goal in front of 2,250 fans. The next foreign team to visit the city were the Denmark under-21 side, who lost 2-0 to the U's. Greek side Panionios came to play in the Bill Halsey Memorial Cup at the Manor on July 31st 1998. Nicky Banger, a Giorgios Mitsiopoulos own goal, and a Phil Gilchrist strike gave the U's a 3-1 win in front of 3,080 spectators.

UNITED IN EUROPE

OXFORD'S only venture into European competition was in the Anglo-Italian Cup in 1972/73. United, placed in Group B, opened with a visit to Bologna on February 22nd 1973. The game, at the Stadio Renato Dall' Ara, was watched by 15,000, but ended goalless, mainly due to some excellent good first-half saves by Amos Adani, and David Roberts' goal-line clearance from Giuseppe Savoldi. In the second half, Hugh Curran hit the bar. Oxford's next game was at home to Torino on March 28th. A crowd of 8,202 saw Derek Clarke head home a Nigel Cassidy cross on the half hour. However, with eight minutes remaining, Rosario Rampanti beat two defenders and goalkeeper Kevin Thomas to level the scores. Next, Oxford visited the Stadio Olimpico to take on AS Roma on April 4th. Hugh Curran scored both goals as Oxford beat the Italian giants 2-0 in front of 4,653. United's final game was at home to Como on May 2nd, where 4,603 were present to witness Dave Roberts score the only goal of the game. These results left Oxford third in the English side of the group – above Fulham but below Blackpool and Newcastle United – while Bologna topped the Italian ranking. In the English semi-final Newcastle beat Crystal Palace 5-1 on aggregate to set up a final against Fiorentina, who beat Bologna 3-2 on aggregate. In the final, played in Florence, Newcastle won 2-1. The U's also took part in a new Anglo-Italian Cup in 1992/93, but only played English opposition, losing 3-1 at home to Swindon Town, and 2-0 at Brentford as they failed to progress beyond the qualifying round. It was the same story the following season, when a 2-1 defeat at Bristol City was followed by a 2-0 home defeat to Portsmouth.

UNTIED IN EUROPE

AFTER winning the 1986 Milk Cup, Oxford were denied the privilege of competing in Europe the following season because of the Heysel disaster on May 29th 1985, which resulted in English teams being banned from Europe until 1990/91. The 1986/87 Uefa Cup was won by IFK Goteborg, who beat Dundee United 2-1 on aggregate in the final. Other clubs United could have faced include: Borussia Monchengladbach, FC Swarovski Tirol, Torino, Inter Milan, Barcelona, Vitoria Setubal, Beveren, Rangers, Bayer Uerdingen, KAA Gent, Spartak Moscow, FC Groningen, Hajduk Split, and Dukla Prague.

THE TRICK IS IN THE HAT

SINCE United became a professional club in 1949, they have scored a total of 70 hat-tricks. Of these, 39 were scored in Southern League days, 31 while United were a Football League club, and two since relegation to the Conference. The first was scored by United's first full-time professional player, Jack Casley, on September 22nd 1949 in a 4-2 win over Guildford City at the Manor. Peter Buchanan became the first man to perform the feat twice, scoring three in an incredible 6-5 win over Gravesend & Northfleet on April 17th 1950, and then another treble on October 5th 1950 as Headington beat Dartford 5-1. Bill Rowstron repeated the feat that same season, with two threesomes, in a 4-1 win at Chelmsford (becoming the first United player to score a hat-trick away from home) in October, and a Boxing Day 4-1 win at Bedford. Ken Smith became the first player to score three hat-tricks, his first coming in a 3-2 win at Bath City on August 22nd 1953, followed by two the following season, at Merthyr Tydfil and against Gravesend. Fred Cotton was the first United player to score a hat-trick in a defeat, his trio coming in a 4-3 home loss to Dartford on March 26th 1958. Geoff Denial scored three hat-tricks in the 1959/60 season, two of them against Cambridge City, and the following season Tony Jones scored three hat-tricks. Bud Houghton then became the first player to score four hat-tricks, beginning with an 8-2 win over Gravesend on April 8th 1961, and followed by three the next season. Alan Willey scored Oxford's first hat-trick as a Football League club, getting all the goals as the U's beat Mansfield on April 27th 1963. Four years after scoring his third hat-trick, Tony Jones grabbed another in a 4-0 win over Wrexham in April 1965. John Aldridge scored four hat-tricks, in 5-2 wins over Leeds United and Oldham Athletic in 1984/85, and also against Ipswich Town when Oxford came back from 3-0 down to win 4-3 on November 23rd 1985. Paul Moody is the only player to have scored five hat-tricks, the first four coming in his first spell at the club, including one in the 9-1 win over Dorchester in November 1995, and his last in the 6-1 win over Halifax in December 2001. Rob Duffy scored Oxford's first Conference hat-trick, in a 5-1 win at Forest Green Rovers, and the last one was James Constable's against Chester in August 2009, although this was later expunged.

MANOR THE MOMENT

HEADINGTON United's first game at the Manor was on September 26th 1925, an Oxfordshire Senior League fixture against Deddington. The visitors were late arriving as their coach had broken down, but when they eventually appeared United's president, Major Melville Lee, performed the ceremonial kick-off. Unfortunately, the visitors weren't in the party mood and won 2-1, with Headington's historic goal scored by E. Grain. Headington drew their next two home games and were then beaten by Thame in the Oxon Charity Cup. Their first home win came on November 21st in the Oxfordshire Senior League, when they avenged their defeat the previous week by beating Thame 8-2. Oxford's last game at the Manor was on May 1st 2001, when United, already relegated to Division Three, drew 1-1 with Port Vale. Andy Scott scored the club's last goal at the ground, before a crowd of 7,080. Before moving to the Manor, United had played for three seasons at the Paddock, further down Osler Road on land adjacent to Headington Manor itself.

MOVING ON

OXFORD'S first game at the Kassam Stadium, so named by chairman Firoz Kassam as a signal of his intent to remain at the club for the long term, was a Bill Halsey Memorial Cup game against Crystal Palace on August 4th 2001. The game was watched by over 7,000 people, despite the South Stand upper tier and executive boxes not having received a safety certificate and remaining closed. Paul Powell scored in a 1-1 draw, with the U's winning the cup 5-4 in the penalty shoot-out. The first competitive game was a Third Division match against Rochdale on August 11th. Jamie Brooks scored for Oxford, but United lost 2-1 before an 8,842 crowd.

THREE'S A CROWD

THE biggest attendance at the Manor was 22,750 for the FA Cup quarter-final against Preston North End on February 29th 1964. This was 1,050 more than for the fifth round tie against Blackburn Rovers two weeks earlier. The best Football League attendance at the ground was 18,740 against Birmingham City on March 31st 1972, beating the 17,939 who watched United lose 2-0 to Derby County on March 22nd 1969.

THREE'S NOT A CROWD

THE lowest Football League crowd at the Manor was 2,526 against Chester City on November 15th 1980, while the lowest recorded attendance for a competitive game was 1,055 for a Zenith Data Systems Cup tie against Portsmouth on December 12th 1990. However, there were a large number of games during the 1950s for which the attendance is unrecorded. The lowest home attendance at the Kassam Stadium is currently 1,508, for Oxford's 0–0 draw with Tonbridge Angels in the FA Trophy on December 15th 2007.

KAS CROWDS

THE best attendance for a Kassam Stadium game is currently the 12,243 who were present for Oxford's last game in the Football League before relegation to the Conference, a 3–2 defeat by Orient. Strangely, the lowest crowd at the stadium at that time was against the same opponents the same season, 1,521 watching an LDV Vans Trophy game won 1–0 by United. On May 3rd 2010 United achieved the best attendance for a Conference game (other than a play-off final) when 11,963 watched the play-off semi-final second leg against Rushden.

OXFORD ALL-IRELAND XI

		Kearns		
Quinn	Rogan		Collins	Langan
Gaston	Magilton		Houghton	Sloan
	Aldridge		Hamilton	

SOME CORNER OF A FOREIGN FIELD

AS far as can be ascertained, United have been relatively lucky when it comes to players who have died while on active service. I can find no record of any U's players who fell during either World War I or World War II. The only player on record to have laid down his life for his country is W. J. Smith, who was one of ten Headington players called up to fight the Boer War in South Africa in 1900, forcing the side to withdraw from the Oxfordshire District League. Smith was described as 'probably the finest back ever seen in junior football'.

A CITY UNITED

THE closest club to United, both literally and metaphorically, is Oxford City. After its initial formation in 1882, City was reformed at a meeting at the Three Cups Hotel in Queen Street on Tuesday 17th October 1893, just ten days before Headington FC were established. The first game between the clubs took place on September 24th 1898, at City's White House Road ground, and it ended with an easy win for Headington, who beat the City 'A' team 5-1 with a hat-trick from A. Ashmore and a brace from Harold Knowles. The sides played a return friendly at Headington's Britannia Field ground, with City 'A' winning 2-1. The first competitive meetings took place the following season in the Oxford & District League, with a goalless draw at White House Road and a 3-3 draw in Headington, with Ashmore scoring two more goals, along with one from J. Fletcher. Another friendly, on January 10th 1903, ended goalless in Headington, and on November 11th 1911 Headington (now sporting the United suffix) shocked the local football scene with a 3-2 win over the City 'A' team, City now having become established as one of the leading amateur sides in the south of England; Phillips (2) and Burke were the scorers. The next meeting was another friendly, on March 7th 1925, when United beat Oxford City Casuals 4-2. Headington's first meeting with the Oxford City first team was in the Amateur Cup first qualifying round on October 10th 1925, when 3,000 spectators saw City win 6-0 at White House Road. United partially atoned in a friendly against City's reserves on March 20th 1926, with a 3-0 win. Another Amateur Cup first round tie at City, on October 12th 1929, was won 3-0 by the Hoops, while their reserves knocked United out of the Oxfordshire Senior Cup 4-0 in Headington on January 25th 1930. The next season Webb scored the only goal as United knocked City out of the Oxon Charity Cup, but on April 6th 1931 City's reserves beat United 8-3 in the final of the Senior Cup. However, in January 1935 United won 4-3 to knock City out of the Senior Cup in the first round, thanks to a Margetts hat-trick. United's best win so far came on December 31st 1938, when they beat City reserves 8-1 in the Charity Cup semi-final, Charlie Machin scoring five. To add insult to injury, United also knocked City reserves out of the Senior Cup in the semi-final, Machin scoring the only goal.

UNITED were to have played City in the extra-preliminary round of the FA Cup in September 1939, but the outbreak of World War II scuppered that and City beat Headington 4-0 in the friendly they arranged instead. In April 1942 they met at White House Road in the Senior Cup final; Percy Blake's goal was not enough as City won 2-1. Headington's first home game after the war was an 8-1 friendly win over City reserves, whom they beat 7-4 in the opening Senior League fixture the following week. However, City's first team wreaked their vengeance in that season's Senior Cup final, beating United 4-0 in front of a record crowd of 6,788 on Easter Monday. Headington's first major win over City came on March 29th 1948, when Jack Ramsden's goal earned a 1-0 win at Iffley Road in the Senior Cup final, watched by 7,796, another record attendance for the competition. Six weeks later Bill Pringle's goal gave Headington victory in the Oxford Hospital Cup final, with 6,500 at White House Road, leading the Oxfordshire FA chairman, Herbert Smith, to declare that Headington were now the senior club in Oxford. The final meeting before United turned professional was a Senior Cup semi-final on April 18th 1949, which City won 2-1 before an Iffley Road crowd of 7,064. The sides played each other in the FA Cup preliminary round in September 1951, United winning the replay 3-0 in front of 8,600 at White House Road, after a 2-2 draw at the Manor, where 8,263 were present. They met again in the FA Cup second qualifying round on October 5th 1957 at City's ground, with United winning 2-0 before a crowd of 9,123, the biggest crowd to watch the derby fixture. The final first-team competitive meeting was on October 4th 1958 in the FA Cup second qualifying round, United winning 3-2 before a Manor crowd of 6,000. After turning professional, United continued to play City regularly in the Senior Cup, although now it was the U's who fielded their reserves, Headington winning the first meeting 2-1 in the semi-final in January 1950. Another 2-1 semi-final win for United came on April 27th 1987, and in the Senior Cup final on April 19th 2005, a Billy Beechers brace and a Craig Davies goal gave United a 3-1 win before a modest crowd of 672. The last time the teams met in a competitive game was on March 3rd 2010, when United won 2-1 at City in the Senior Cup semi-final.

UP FOR THE CUP

HEADINGTON United's first game in the FA Cup was on September 5th 1931, when they lost 8-2 at home to Hounslow in the extra preliminary round. The following season they drew 2-2 at Bicester Town in the preliminary round, losing the replay 4-2 at the Manor. United's first win in the cup came on September 4th 1937, when they beat Marlow 4-2 thanks to a Sansom hat-trick. However, in the next round Osberton Radiators won 2-1 at the Manor to eliminate Headington. United were avenged the following season, beating the Radiators 5-2 away in the extra preliminary round. They then beat Henley Town away 5-2 before losing 3-2 to Windsor & Eton at the Manor. United's first FA Cup game after World War II was an embarrassing 8-1 defeat at Banbury Spencer, but in 1946/47 they had their best cup run yet, winning 3-2 at Bicester, beating Banbury Spencer 3-2, and then winning at Aylesbury, also 3-2. The run ended with a 5-2 defeat at Uxbridge in the third preliminary round.

GIANTS KILLED

AS a Football League side, Oxford were knocked out of the FA Cup by non-league opposition seven times. First was in a second round replay in January 1967, when Southern League Bedford won 1-0 after a 1-1 Manor draw. The following season Chelmsford, also of the Southern League, needed two replays to eliminate United in the second round. Both the drawn games had ended 3-3, but Chelmsford won 1-0 at Brentford's Griffin Park. In November 1976, another Southern League club, Kettering, beat Oxford 1-0 at the Manor, with player-manager Derek Dougan scoring the goal, after a 1-1 draw at Rockingham Road. Almost exactly a year later Nuneaton Borough, another Southern League outfit, won 2-0 in the first round, and two years later it was the turn of Isthmian League side Barking to beat the U's, with a 1-0 first round win. However, the worst humiliation occurred on November 13th 1994 when Oxford, top of the Third Division, visited Marlow, who were in the Isthmian League Premier Division relegation zone. Marlow, featuring United old boys Peter Rhoades-Brown and Les Phillips, and managed by Peter Foley, won 2-0 with goals from John Caesar. The last time United fell to non-league opponents was December 9th 2000, when Conference side Chester City won 3-2 after United led 2-0.

AMATEURISH IN THE EXTREME

ON September 30th 1922, Headington United played their first FA Amateur Cup tie. This was also the club's first game in a national competition, even though the early stages were played on a very much local basis. The first opponents were St. Frideswide, from Osney, in the first preliminary round, and the game ended 2-2 with Baskerville and Adams on target for the Headingtonians. The following week United won the replay 4-0; Adams, Spindler, Vallis, and Durran scoring to set up a second preliminary round tie at Newbury, which the Berkshire side won 6-1. The following season Headington again failed at the second preliminary round, losing 2-0 at Morris Motors having beaten Witney Town 2-1 at home in the previous round. In fact, in every season prior to World War II, United failed to get past the second preliminary round of this tournament, with results that included a 6-0 defeat at Oxford City on October 10th 1925, a 7-0 defeat at Newbury just over a year later, a 6-1 loss at Windsor & Eton the next season, a 4-1 defeat at Caversham St. Andrews in October 1928, a 7-1 home defeat by Marlow in 1932, an 8-2 home defeat by Slough two seasons later, the same result at Marlow the following season, and a 4-1 defeat at Banbury Spencer in 1936. It looked like the ending of the war would see an upturn in United's Amateur Cup fortunes, as they beat Pressed Steel 4-1 in the preliminary round in September 1945, followed by a 3-1 win over Windsor & Eton and a 5-3 victory over Marlow in extra time of the third qualifying round. However, that Marlow game was abandoned shortly before the end because of bad light, and the match was scheduled to be replayed in Marlow a week later, Headington losing 6-2 with Charlie Machin being sent off. Marlow proved Headington's nemesis again the following season, beating United 2-0 after the U's had despatched Henley Town 5-1 in the first preliminary round. In 1947 United beat Abingdon 5-2, and Aylesbury 2-0, before being knocked out by Reading biscuit-makers Huntley & Palmer's in the second preliminary round, before a Manor crowd of 3,000. United's last season as an amateur club again saw them fare poorly in this competition, losing 4-1 at home to Slough in the third preliminary round, having beaten Wallingford 6-1 in the previous round.

JOEY BEAUCHAMP ON THE WING

IF there's one single player, more than anyone else, who people associate with Oxford United – especially in modern times – it's Joey Beauchamp. The exciting winger was born in Oxford and as a youngster played for Summertown Stars. He was selected to be one of the ball boys for United's Milk Cup triumph in 1986, and the following year he was signed by Oxford on YTS forms. His first game was as a substitute for Lee Nogan against Watford in a 4-0 defeat on the last day of the 1988/89 season, when he had just turned 18. He had a five-game loan spell at Swansea City, where he scored twice and had the Welsh side trying to sign him. United wisely refused and Joey went on to become an Oxford legend. He scored his first goal for Oxford in a 3-0 win over Sunderland on December 28th 1991, and had scored 23 goals by the time that West Ham United bid £1 million for him. With Oxford having just been relegated to the Third Division the bid was accepted, and Joey signed for the Hammers with the proviso that he could continue to live in Oxford, where he was buying a house. However, West Ham wanted him to move to London and after he played just one game for them, a friendly at Oxford City, he was sold to Swindon for £800,000 (including Adrian Whitbread), just 58 days after joining the east Londoners. Joey's time at Swindon was unhappy, especially after Steve McMahon replaced John Gorman as manager, and 16 months after he left, Oxford bought Joey back for just £75,000. Beauchamp immediately re-established himself as a crowd favourite, scoring the third goal as Oxford beat Swindon 3-0 and weighing in with some vital goals in United's promotion push, including a 35-yard dipping volley against Blackpool that many consider to be the best goal scored at the Manor. Readers of the Oxford fanzine *Rage On* voted Joey as the best player of the 1990s, and Joey turned down big money moves to Nottingham Forest, Reading, and Southampton to stay at the Manor. This didn't particularly enamour him to the board, who were desperate for cash, but consolidated his reputation among the fans. An injury to his big toe eventually ended his career, which he signed off with a superb volley against Exeter City at the Kassam Stadium on February 23rd 2002. Joey went on to play for Didcot, Abingdon Town, and Sunday League outfit Oxford Yellows.

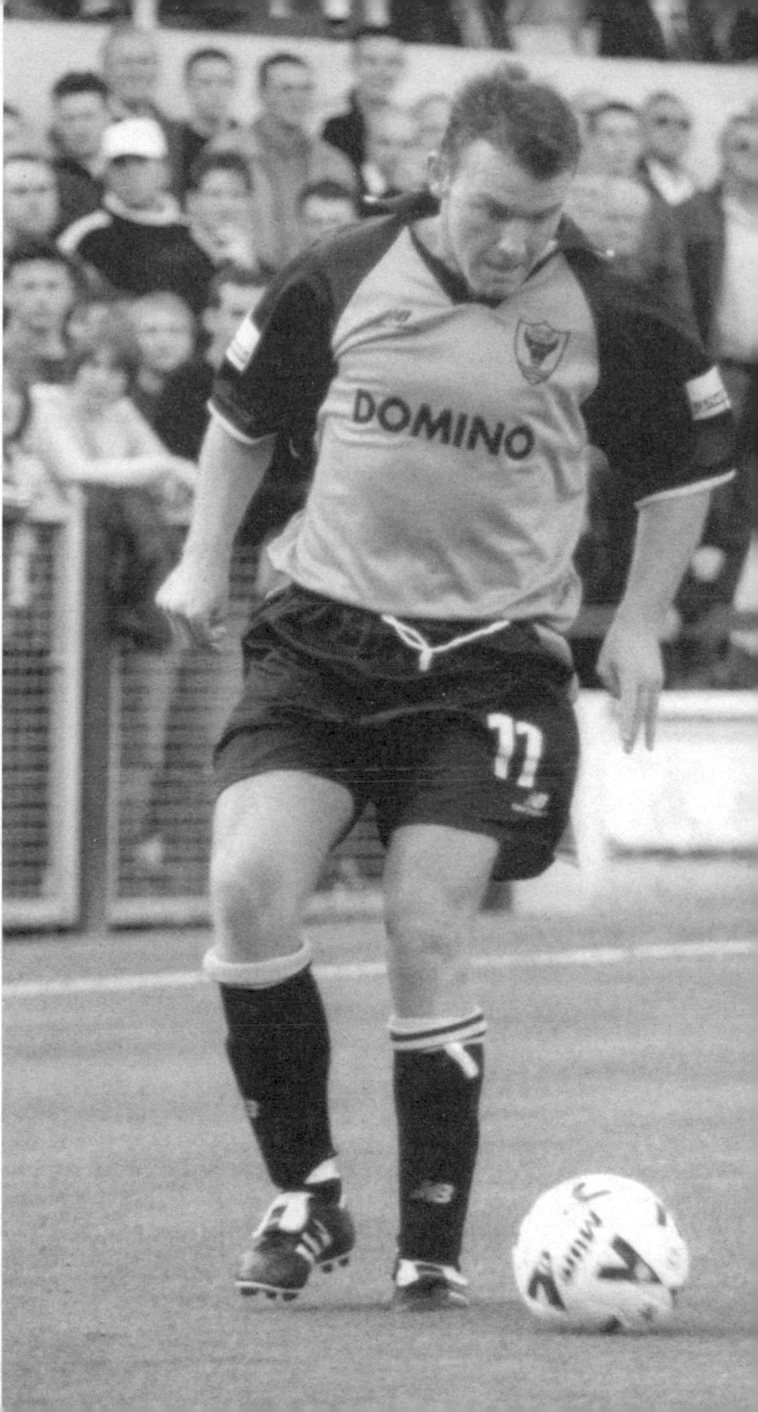

JOEY BEAUCHAMP, UNITED'S PLAYER OF THE 1990S

FAT CHANCE

OXFORD'S record in the FA Trophy is almost as poor as Headington's in the Amateur Cup. In their first season in the Trophy, 2006/07, United needed a replay to beat Lewes 1-0 before being knocked out 2-1 by Halifax in a replay. The following season Tonbridge Angels humbled the Yellows 1-0 after drawing 0-0 at the Kassam Stadium. In 2008/09 Oxford were beaten 2-1 at home by York City, having won 2-0 at AFC Sudbury in the previous round. Their best season was 2009/10, when they beat Hayes & Yeading 1-0 in the first round, Woking 1-0 in the second round, then won 3-1 at Chelmsford before being knocked out 2-1 by Kidderminster in the quarter-finals.

EVERYWHERE WE GO

WHEN Luton Town visited the Kassam Stadium on September 8th 2009, the sides set a new record. Oxford won the game 2-0 with goals from James Constable and Jamie Cook, but of greater significance was the fact that United and Luton became the first clubs to meet in each of the top five divisions of English football. The clubs' first meeting was in Division Two (now the Championship) on September 1st 1970, Luton winning 4-0 at Kenilworth Road. On October 12th 1985 the Hatters visited the Manor for a Division One (now the Premiership) game that ended 1-1, with Trevor Hebberd scoring for Oxford. The sides met in the Third Division (now League One) on September 25th 1999, when Luton won 4-2, and on September 8th 2001 an Andy Scott goal earned United a 1-1 draw in Bedfordshire in a fourth tier (League Two) encounter. The game that took place exactly eight years later was the clubs' first meeting in the Conference Premier Division. In addition the sides have also met in the League Cup, the Full Members Cup, and the Associate Members Cup.

UNITED SCOTLAND XI

McCaldon

McDonald   Elliott   McGuckin   Kinniburgh

McGrogan   Lilley   Perry   Heron

McCulloch   Curran

ORIENTAL TRIAL

UNITED often have trialists playing for the reserves, or in friendlies, who never make it to the first team. Two particularly exotic gentlemen played for the reserves in a 5-2 win over Bristol Rovers on August 26th 1987. The duo had arrived from Japan, hoping to make their way in the English game, and the afternoon's biggest cheer was reserved for PA announcer Bob Wyllie when he annunciated perfectly central defender Takao Nonaka's substitution for Toshimitsu Yoshikoshi in the 61st minute. Neither player scored, as Oxford's goals came from Sean Reck with the first and fifth, Dean Saunders, Lee Nogan, and full-back Robbie Williams.

THE PEN IS MIGHTIER

A NUMBER of people with connections to United have committed their stories to print. At board level, former chairman Vic Couling published *Anatomy of a Football Club* in 1983, documenting his time at the club from his first involvement in 1947. Managers to have appeared in print are Jim Smith, who has had two autobiographies published: *Bald Eagle* in 1990 and *The Autobiography* in 2000 (re-titled *It's Only a Game* when released in paperback two years later). Mark Lawrenson published his autobiography, also nattily titled *The Autobiography*, in 1988, before he became Maurice Evans' successor, and Denis Smith released *Just One of Seven* in October 2008. Joe Kinnear had *Still Crazy* published in 2000, before he was appointed as a so-called director of football at United. Assistant manager to Mark Wright, Ted McMinn, wrote *The Ted McMinn Story*, which also came out in October 2008. A month earlier *To Be Honest* was released, about Graham Rix. Players, too, have produced literary endeavours, with Ted Croker first to the typewriter with his autobiography *The First Voice You Will Hear Is...* which hit the streets in 1987. Ron Atkinson, unsurprisingly, has had a lot of words written about him, including *United to Win* (1984) and *Big Ron: A Different Ball Game* (1998). John Aldridge published his autobiography, *My Story*, in 1999; goalkeeper Jimmy Glass's biography *One Hit Wonder*, by Roger Lytollis, appeared in September 2004; and Dean Windass wrote *Deano: From Gypsyville to the Premiership* in October 2007. Former chairman Robert Maxwell has had a number of books written about him, including *The Outsider* in 1992, *Foreign Body* in 1996, *Israel's Superspy* in 2003, and *The Final Verdict* in 2008.

LIKE FATHER, LIKE SON

ONE of the worst cases of nepotism in football concerns Oxford United. When, to the surprise of absolutely everybody, Argentine manager Ramon Díaz became manager of the club in December 2004 there followed an influx of foreign players. Notable arrivals included Uruguayan defender Mateo Corbo, Argentinean midfielder Lucas Cominelli, and his compatriot Juan Pablo Raponi. Also joining Oxford were Díaz's two sons, Michael and Emiliano. Michael never played a first-team game for the U's, and it was his older brother who made it into the Football League, coming on as a substitute for Raponi in a home defeat by Grimsby on March 5th 2005. Emiliano was nominally a right winger, although his actual performances suggested that football might not be his main vocation. Michael, on the other hand, was certainly full-blooded in the tackle, to the extent that even in training he had to be restrained, and allegedly it was his tackle that led to Jamie Brooks' prolonged injury just as he was due for a comeback. When Ramon left Oxford he took his sons with him, and they followed his father to San Lorenzo, in Buenos Aires. After Ramon left for Club America in Mexico the sons went to San Luis. Both Michael and Emiliano had trials with Italian first division (group B) club Benevento, and Emi had an unsuccessful trial at Major League Soccer clubs DC United and New York Red Bulls. Most recently, Emiliano was playing for Argentine side All Boys, in the National B Division, while Michael moved to Defensores de Belgrano (Primera B Metropolitana), with their father Ramon apparently paying their wages!

PLANS FOR NIGEL

NIGEL Winterburn never played a first-team game for Oxford, although he did come on as a substitute for David Grant in a 4-3 friendly win at Worcester City on August 13th 1983; his performance inspired the *Oxford Mail* to opine that he looked out of his depth. Winterburn joined the U's from Birmingham City, for whom he also never played in the first team, on trial in July 1983, but by the time the season had started at the end of August he had already moved on to Wimbledon. In 1987 he moved to Arsenal, and he won the first of his two England caps in 1987, as a substitute against Italy.

JEWS FOR THE U'S

THE only Jewish professional player to have played for United is Josh Kennet, a stylish midfielder who came up through the United youth team ranks. Before that, he spent time at Millwall and Spurs, and it was after the latter opted not to sign him that he went for a trial at Oxford, who were impressed with what they saw and signed him on YTS terms, offering him a short-term professional contract two years later. Kennet also made a few appearances for London Maccabi Lions in the Maccabi Southern Football League. He made his Oxford debut, his only appearance for the club, on New Year's Day 2007 away to Exeter City, coming on for Rufus Brevett. Unfortunately, he was released at the end of that season, and left to play for Maccabi Herzliya in Israel.

WHAT'S IN A NAME?

ELVEY, Vellenzer, Symington, Cunningham, Baron, and Larmouth all played for United, although you wouldn't recognise them from their names. Elvey was one of Stan Aldous's middle names (his other was Reginald). Aldous played five games after joining from Orient in 1955, where he was captain for seven seasons, but injury forced him to retire and he joined Headington's coaching staff. Vellenzer was the middle name of Jon Narbett, a midfielder who was signed from Hereford United by Brian Horton and who left for Swedish side Kalmar without making a huge impression. Peter Symington Buchanan was a former Scotland player, who scored on his only international appearance, against Czechoslovakia in 1937. He played for Chelsea before the war, joining Headington from Brentford in September 1949. Andrew Cunningham Bodel was another Scot, a central defender who came up through United's youth ranks. He left to play for Oxford City, after 141 games for the U's, in the late 1970s. George Baron Luke was a centre-forward who played 24 games with United during the year from October 1960, scoring nine goals. George Larmouth Forrester was born in Cannock and played only six games for Headington, during the 1956/57 season; he died in 1981. One of Dexter Blackstock's middle names is Titus, but his only first-team game for United was a substitute appearance in a pre-season friendly against Spurs. He moved to Southampton in 2003, earning United £275,000 in compensation despite never having played a competitive game for the first team.

ON THE BUSES

ON November 15th 1986, Oxford United visited Loftus Road for a top-flight game. Ray Houghton gave United a deserved lead, but future U John Byrne equalised for QPR in the final minute. At precisely 5.30, on the orders of manager Maurice Evans, the Oxford team coach departed, leaving behind seven players who weren't ready on time. The players concerned were John Aldridge, Kevin Brock, Jeremy Charles, Steve Hardwick, Les Phillips, Peter Rhoades-Brown, and captain Malcolm Shotton, all of whom had to make their own way back to Oxford. Aldridge, who had made no secret of his wish to move to a 'bigger' club, threatened to put in a transfer request, although the following Monday Evans apologised to the players and the threat was withdrawn. Nevertheless, this was a damaging mistake by Evans, and two months later Aldridge moved to Liverpool for £750,000.

FIRST PROS

UNITED'S first professional players, other than player-coach Harold Thompson, were Cliff Nugent and Peter Sharman. Both were on Oxford City's books when, in August 1949, they approached Headington to sign as professionals. The Headington board suggested they think it over before making the step up from the Isthmian League, but both players returned to sign as part-time professionals. The first that Oxford City knew of the matter was when they read the local press the following day. Nugent started badly, disappointing in the pre-season trials and then pulling a groin muscle that kept him out for seven weeks. He came back on the left wing for the reserves, but started his Southern League career on the right. After switching back to outside-left he became an automatic choice. The following season he was so successful that he had trials with Wolves, Fulham, Orient, West Bromwich, Aston Villa, West Ham United, Leeds United, and Cardiff City, who he joined in February 1951 for £2,500, a Southern League record, after their initial bid of £2,000 was rejected. Nugent was born in London, coming to Oxford when he was posted to Cowley Barracks with the Royal Army Pay Corps. He joined Oxford City after demobilisation. Sharman, on the other hand, was from Wolvercote and was working in Banbury when he joined Headington. He never adjusted to the pace of the Southern League and, after moving to live in Burford, he asked for his contract to be terminated in September 1950.

MAXWELL'S CHOPPER

OXFORD United's AGM in 1986 was possibly the shortest on record. It was due to start at 12 noon on a Thursday, awkward enough, but chairman Robert Maxwell arrived early and, despite the protests from his fellow board members, started proceedings well before noon. He rattled through the agenda and the meeting was finished less than five minutes after it had started. Maxwell left the room as bemused shareholders were arriving and made his way to his helicopter, waiting in the centre-circle on the Manor pitch. Before flying off to Edinburgh to visit that year's Commonwealth Games – sponsored by his Mirror Group Newspapers – and much to the disgust of groundsman Mick Moore, Maxwell urinated in the centre of the pitch.

UNITED WALES XI

Rouse

Slatter	Melville	Roberts	Ricketts
Wright	Folland	Haldane	Charles
	Saunders	Davies	

ONE, TWO, THREE, OFF!

WHEN United visited Blackpool on February 21st 1976, they equalled Plymouth Argyle's Football League record for the most dismissals, as three players were given their marching orders by referee Peter Richardson. Skipper John Shuker was the first to go after committing two bookable fouls, both on Billy Ronson. This was the first time that Shuker had been sent off in his career and, with the U's down to ten men, Blackpool took the lead a minute before half-time. United were already 2-0 down by the time Mick Tait, in his first season as a professional, was sent off, also for a foul on Ronson. Right at the end Peter Houseman joined his teammates in the dressing room for decking Alan Ainscow after the Blackpool player allegedly spat in his face. This was Houseman's first sending off in his lengthy career. United later wrote to Blackpool and the FA to apologise for their behaviour, while a disciplinary committee banned Shuker and Houseman for one game and Tait for two.

MORE CLUBS THAN JACK NICKLAUS

JEFFERSON Louis has played for more clubs in his career than any other United player. Gainsborough Trinity became his 21st club when he joined them in June 2010. Having started his career at Aylesbury West Indies, after he was released from prison, he was given his first proper chance by Lee Sinnott, then manager of Thame, who recommended him to Oxford. He had loan spells at Woking and Gravesend while at Oxford, where he spent two years, before leaving for Forest Green Rovers. He rejoined Woking after just eight games and then had a brief spell at Bristol Rovers in 2005, during which year he also appeared for Hemel Hempstead, Lewes, Worthing, and Stevenage Borough. He scored six goals in 18 games at Broadhall Way before leaving for Eastleigh and then to Yeading, before he found himself at Havant & Waterlooville. He then joined Weymouth, and after a three-game spell at Maidenhead he returned to the league with Mansfield Town in January 2008, but they were relegated that season. Louis remained in the Conference but with Wrexham, where he stayed for a whole season before joining Crawley Town. It was from there that he joined Rushden on loan.

THE CONFERENCE CENTRE

THE Conference started life in 1979 as the Alliance Premier League, becoming the Gola League in 1984 and the GM Vauxhall Conference two years later. In 1998 it was the Nationwide Conference and the Blue Square Conference in 2007. Since its inception, five of the top six attendance records (excluding play-off finals) have been set by Oxford:

11,963	Oxford United v. Rushden & Diamonds	(03/05/10)
	Play-Off semi-final	
11,065	Oxford United v. Woking	(26/12/06)
10,803	Carlisle United v. Aldershot	(06/05/05)
	Play-Off semi-final	
10,691	Oxford United v. Exeter City	(08/05/07)
	Play-Off semi-final	
10,613	Oxford United v. Luton Town	(08/09/09)
10,298	Oxford United v. Northwich Victoria	(26/04/09)

The attendance of 42,669 for the 2010 Play-Off final against York was a record for the competition.

DECLINE AND FALL

IN the 1997/98 season, Oxford finished 12th in the second tier, or 32nd in the national football Pyramid. They have yet to reach those heights again and, apart from one season, they have finished successively lower every year until 2009. In 1999 Oxford were 43rd overall as they were relegated to the third tier; in 2000 United avoided the drop to the fourth tier by one place as they finished 64th, but they ended the 2000/01 season bottom, in 68th place. Their first season back in the basement saw the U's struggle, finishing the season 89th in the Pyramid, although the one blip in the club's decline followed as they finished 76th in 2003, just one place below the play-offs. They finished one place lower the following season and then dropped to 83rd before ending the 2005/06 season in their lowest league position, 91st in the Pyramid and relegated to the Conference. In their first season back in non-league, Oxford finished three places lower than in 2006, in second place, or 94th overall, and fell even further the following year when they ended 101st, their lowest finish since 1959. The arrival of Chris Wilder halted the fall, and in 2009 United finished seventh in the Conference, or 99th in the Pyramid.

NOT ENOUGH COOKS

CELEBRITY chef Gordon Ramsay clearly feels that being associated with Oxford United is a good career move. Ramsay played at left-back in a few games for Banbury United, but he also claimed, in an interview with the *Evening Standard* in 1998, that United scouts spotted him while he played for Warwickshire in a county match when he was 15, and during an FA Youth Cup game against Arsenal he was spotted by Glasgow Rangers scouts. However, United have never played Arsenal in an FA Youth Cup match, and there are no contemporary records that show Ramsay ever played for Oxford. Similarly, Rangers experts ridiculed his claims that he played three first-team games for them before injury ended his career. Ramsay repeated his claims about playing for Oxford on BBC Radio Four's *Desert Island Discs* in 2002. He later issued a statement claiming that; "Any inaccuracies regarding the details of this period can be explained by the fact that all this occurred nearly 25 years ago."

PARTY AT THE PALACE

OXFORD and Crystal Palace have met each other in the league in eight different seasons, in each of which one of the clubs has been either promoted or relegated. The first meeting was on November 9th 1968, United's first in the Second Division, when Palace won 2-0, followed in March by a 1-1 draw at Selhurst Park; the Glaziers (as they were) finished the season in second place and won promotion to the top flight. Five years later Palace were back in Division Two and the sides fought out the same set of results, with the venues reversed, and again it was Palace who changed divisions with relegation to the Third. In 1976/77, Oxford joined Palace in Division Three, drawing 2-2 at Selhurst Park and losing 1-0 at the Manor as the south London side won promotion back to the Second Division. Oxford's 1,000th Football League game was on December 29th 1984, when Crystal Palace were thrashed 5-0 at the Manor, although they won the return fixture with a Trevor Aylott goal; United won promotion to the top flight that season. Three years later they met again, both sides winning 1-0 at home as the U's were relegated to Division Two. In 1993/94 both sides swapped divisions, as Palace were promoted to the top flight, doing the double over relegated United. Three years later both sides were back in the second tier, Oxford losing 4-1 at home to the Londoners after a 2-2 draw in Norwood. Palace finished sixth, but were promoted via the play-offs. The sides' final meetings were in 1998/99 when Palace again did the double over Oxford, who finished in the second-tier relegation zone.

LEAP LIKE A SALMON

MIKE Salmon is, statistically, without doubt the worst goalkeeper ever to turn out for United. He played just one game for the club while on loan from Charlton Athletic, on December 12th 1998 at the Manor. Birmingham City won 7-1, with 7,189 witnessing the humiliation. To be fair to Salmon, who returned to the Valley the following day, only four of the goals could be directly attributable to his errors, as the Blues stormed into a 4-0 half-time lead and added three more strikes in the second half. The biggest cheer of the day was reserved for Dean Windass's last-minute consolation goal.

GREAVES THE DEPARTED

WHEN Ian Greaves replaced Bill Asprey, Oxford were third from bottom of Division Three. In his first game, on Boxing Day 1980, United beat leaders Charlton Athletic 1-0. This started a revival that led the U's to a 14th-place finish. Next season Greaves, who wasn't on a contract, resigned in February to join Wolves, after Robert Maxwell had misrepresented him in the press, less than a fortnight after leading United to a 3-0 win at First Division Brighton & Hove Albion in the FA Cup fourth round. Greaves, a former Busby Babe at Manchester United, died in January 2009.

GETTING THE BLUES

OXFORD'S 7-1 defeat by Birmingham City on December 12th 1998 was their heaviest at home as a pro club; the first time they had shipped seven at home since losing 8-2 to Abingdon Services in the Oxfordshire Charity Cup on November 8th 1942. That result equalled a defeat by Slough on October 6th 1934 in the FA Amateur Cup first preliminary round, while two years earlier in the second qualifying round of the same tournament, Marlow won 7-1 at the Manor. The previous season, on September 5th, United's first FA Cup experience ended with a home defeat by Hounslow 8-2 in the extra preliminary round. On September 24th 1927, Littlemore beat United 7-2 at the Manor in the Oxfordshire Senior League, but the club's worst home defeat was on February 15th 1908, when Headington lost a City Junior League Division Two game 9-0 to YMCA II.

FIRST BLOOD

WHEN Gary Briggs, nicknamed Rambo by Oxford supporters, joined United from Middlesbrough permanently in July 1978 – following a four-month loan spell – it was at the Football League's first transfer tribunal. Briggs was due to be the second case heard at the sitting, but was swapped with John Lacy, who moved from Fulham to Spurs for £195,000, meaning Briggs was the first player to be transferred under the new system. Oxford had initially offered Boro £30,000 for Briggs, but once the case went to tribunal, the offer was reduced to £12,500, which was the fee that the panel eventually determined. Briggs went on to play at Oxford for over 11 years, making 508 appearances.

CHRISTMAS BABY

THE only player to have appeared for Oxford who was born on Christmas Day is Lucas Cominelli. Lucas was a full-blooded, committed, terror in the midfield; an archetypal ball winner, who didn't mind too much if he took the man as well as the ball. Born in Buenos Aires, and signed from Pahang in Malaysia, he had pedigree with Tenerife, and a flowing Argentinean hairstyle. Although lacking in finesse, he eventually got into the swing of the English game, and at the end of Ramon Díaz's tenure many Oxford fans regretted that Brian Talbot failed to offer him a new contract.

CHRISTMAS CHEER

THE first time that United took to the field on Christmas Day was in 1913, when Thame 'A' were beaten 3-0 in the Oxfordshire Junior League. Seven years later, United lost 3-1 at bitter rivals Cowley in the same competition. By Christmas 1925, the U's had upgraded to the Oxfordshire Senior League, where they met Thame and beat them 4-1. Cowley were the visitors for an Oxfordshire Senior League game in 1934, with Headington winning 2-0, and the following year United beat the same opponents 3-2. In 1936, Banbury Spencer 'A' were beaten 5-3 at the Spencer Stadium and in 1941 a wartime fixture against Oxford City reserves in the Senior League saw United lose 3-0. Pressed Steel were the visitors in 1942, United winning 5-4. Headington's last season in the Senior League featured a Christmas Day visit by St. Frideswide, but United showed no Christmas spirit, sending the Saints packing by winning 6-1. In 1950, United beat Bedford 2-0 at the Manor in the Southern League, and six years later the same opponents beat the U's 2-1 at the Eyrie. The last time that United played on Christmas Day was in 1957, when a visit to Aggborough yielded both points as Kidderminster Harriers were beaten 3-1.

AIN'T NO SANITY CLAUSE

ON December 22nd 1984, United's surge to promotion was suspended at Fratton Park. Kevin Brock gave Oxford the lead, but a Portsmouth fan dressed in a Santa Claus outfit ran onto the pitch. In the time added on for this stoppage, Alan Biley scored twice to earn Pompey the points.

SPONSORS' FORM

UNITED'S first shirt sponsor was the *Sunday Journal*, a newspaper owned by the Free Newspaper Group, whose owner was former club chairman Tony Rosser. The first game at which their name adorned Oxford's shirts was at home to Lincoln City on October 31st 1981. Future sponsors were the *Sunday People*, owned by Robert Maxwell's Mirror Group Newspapers, BPCC (British Printing and Communications Corporation), another Maxwell-owned company; Wang Computers; yet another Maxwell company in Pergamon Press; Unipart, whose nine-year deal was the longest so far; Domino; and Buildbase, who were announced as new shirt sponsors in July 2001. In 2009 United's away shirts were sponsored by Buildbase's sister company, Plumbase. In 2010 Bridle Insurance became the club's sponsors.

ALL-OXFORDSHIRE XI

Kearns

Quartermain	Wanless	Wright	Powell
Beauchamp	Whitehead	Seacole	Allen
	Hackett	Brooks	

Subs: Warrell, Mustoe, Brock, Love, Foley

CITY CHAMPS

HEADINGTON'S first league title was won in 1897/98, in just their fourth season of competitive football. The villagers won the Oxford City Junior League Division 'B' title without losing a game, to set up a final against Division 'A' winners St. Mary Magdalene, who they beat 1-0 in a replay after a 1-1 draw.

	P	W	D	L	F	A	Pts
Headington	**8**	**7**	**1**	**0**	**35**	**2**	**15**
Oxford Temperance	8	5	0	3	26	17	10
Victoria Reserves	8	4	1	3	26	5	9
St. Paul's	8	2	0	6	11	30	4
Oxford Institute	8	1	0	7	6	50	2

GETTING WITH THE PROGRAMME

THE earliest known United programme dates from September 28th 1935, for an Intermediate League game between Headington United reserves and Thame reserves. While this was the side's first home game in this new league, the first team had played Bicester in the Oxfordshire Senior League a week earlier, so it seems reasonable to assume that a programme would also have been issued for this game. The Thame programme is very rare, and it has been valued at around £1,000.

IN THE LINE OF DUTY

PETER Houseman is the only player who has died while on United's books. He and his wife, Sally, and two friends, Alan and Janice Gillham, were killed in a car crash on the A40 as they were driving home to Witney following a dance at the Cowley Workers Social Club, organised by the joint fundraising committee of the Oxford United Football and Supporters Club. The date was March 20th 1977, and Houseman's last game was a 1-0 home defeat by Crystal Palace the day before. The crash left six children orphaned. Houseman had been signed by Oxford from Chelsea for £30,000 in May 1975.

EURO STAR

OXFORD have only once received money for a player from an overseas side. Craig Davies was sold to Italian side Hellas Verona of Serie B for £85,000 in January 2006, 17 months after being signed from the youth team of Manchester City. He made his debut as a substitute against Notts County on August 20th 2004, and Ramon Díaz handed him his first start on December 11th, when he scored against Cambridge United. He made 26 starts and 29 substitute appearances for Oxford and won two Wales caps before he let it be known that he was not going to sign a new contract at the end of the season, after United allegedly spurned an approach for him from Premiership side Charlton Athletic. His time at Verona was an unhappy one, and he made just one appearance for them before they loaned him to Wolverhampton Wanderers for the whole of the 2006/07 season. In June 2007 he returned to England to play for Oldham Athletic after Wolves opted not to make his loan permanent.

QUARRY UNITED

WHEN the club was formed in October 1893 by Dr Robert Hitchings, it was known simply as Headington FC, although the cricket club for which Hitchings and many of the early players played was called Headington United CC. The football club changed its name to Headington United on July 25th 1911, following a meeting at which it was decided to merge with Headington Quarry. Quarry had been formed in September 1907 by members of Strete Temperance and on January 18th 1908, they played a friendly against Headington at Britannia Field, which Headington won 3-0. A rematch was held on January 2nd 1909, at the Quarry Recreation Ground, which Headington won 3-2. On October 8th 1910, the sides met in a competitive fixture for the only time; in the County Junior Shield first round Quarry won 3-0 at the Rec. Another merger took place on August 21st 1913, when the Highfield club amalgamated with Headington United. Highfield were a Thursday League side located in Headington, and this development allowed United to field two teams in the Oxfordshire Thursday League.

SOMETHING FISHY

KENNETH Henry Albert Fish joined Oxford from Birmingham City in 1964 to take on the role of trainer. He was born on February 20th 1914 in Cape Town, South Africa, and joined Port Vale from Aston Villa in November 1937. He became the first player to move from England to Europe when Vale sold him to Young Boys of Bern in October 1938. He returned to Vale shortly before the Second World War, during which he played for Stafford Rangers, returning to Burslem as trainer in 1946. He was caretaker manager at Vale for a couple of months at the end of 1951, and in 1958 he moved to Birmingham as trainer-coach. Mr Fish, as he was known to everyone at United, was a strict disciplinarian and totally dedicated to serving the club; he took on numerous tasks, including masseur and kit launderer. He was rewarded for his time at the club with a testimonial against Leicester City in May 1974 after 10 years' service, and at the Milk Cup final in April 1986, when manager Maurice Evans sent Mr Fish up the famous Wembley steps to receive Evans' winners' medal. He retired in 1988 at the age of 74, and died on August 4th 2005, aged 91.

MONEY FOR NOTHING

OXFORD supporters can be a generous lot, and the club has benefitted greatly from that generosity over the years. The Headington United Supporters Club was inaugurated on September 3rd 1946 in a meeting at the Britannia Inn (the same place where the football club was formed 53 years earlier), with Billy Jewel elected as its first president and Sid Toms as secretary. The Supporters Club was in action almost immediately, providing voluntary labour to help construct a new stand at the Manor upon election to the Southern League in 1949. In October 1949, the Supporters Club offered to pay for covered turnstiles in Manor Road, and in December they loaned the football club £600, which was turned into a gift in May 1950, with an additional £1,500 the following month. In March 1951 the Supporters Club stumped up the £500 required to install permanent floodlighting at the ground. These sums paled into insignificance in 1957, when the Supporters Club contributed more than £33,000 towards the construction of the new Beech Road stand. The Supporters Club lost its independence in 1982, when Robert Maxwell merged it into the football club, but United's fans continued to contribute to the running of the club. In November 1998, with the club close to going into administration and having to pay the players' wages with a grant from the PFA, members of the public delivered food parcels for the backroom staff, who worked without pay for two months. In 2009 various supporters' groups, led by the supporters' trust OxVox, set up a '12th Man' initiative to raise money to go towards new signings. The ambition was to try and raise £10,000 in the first year, but this sum was exceeded within a few months, and funded the signings of players such as Jamie Cook, Onome Sodje, and Anthony Tonkin.

THE REAL THING

IN April 2006, Oxford fan Andy Perrin won £50,000 for United in a competition organised by Coca Cola. Perrin entered the draw every day throughout the 105-day promotion and was one of only three prize winners, with Southampton gaining £250,000 to sign Bradley Wright-Phillips and Brentford also winning £50,000 to go towards striker Chris Moore. The money won by Chinnor-based Perrin was spent on the wages of new skipper Phil Gilchrist, who arrived on a free transfer from Rotherham United.

ON THE PAGE

UNITED have rarely appeared in novels, although they earn a few mentions in Colin Dexter's *Morse* series. However, in Peter Tickler's *Blood On The Cowley Road*, games played at the Kassam Stadium are a significant part of the action and Oxford United feature heavily. There are references to Paul Wanless and Julian Alsop, and fans in the East Stand are crucial to the plot. There is also a solicitor named Basham. Solicitors named after United players continue in Peter's follow-up novel *Blood in Grandpont* and also his third book (a work in progress), which is set during the 2009/10 season, with the central character being a fanatical supporter of the Yellows. Peter refuses to reveal whether any United fans commit murder or are murdered, but he claims that the idea of a serial killer of referees becomes more attractive with every game he watches!

SOMETHING IN RESERVE

UNITED have fielded a reserve side since 1899, when they entered their second XI in the City Junior League 'B', after the first team had their application to join the Oxford & District League accepted. Their first game was a 4-0 defeat at Clarendon Press 2nd, and the second a 10-0 loss at College Servants; that first season was something of a disaster because after the side lost two players called up to fight in the Boer War they were unable to field a team and had to withdraw in January 1900. When Headington joined the Spartan League in 1947, the reserves took their place in the Oxfordshire Senior League, and upon entry to the Southern League two years later the second string were founder members of the Metropolitan League (initially called the Home Counties League until the FA rejected that idea). The first reserve game as a professional outfit was a 2-2 draw at home to West Ham United's 'B' team on September 10th 1949. In 1964/65 Oxford United joined the Football Combination. The side's first game in this competition was at home to Swindon Town, which United won 5-0 in front of 2,488, on August 26th 1964. In 1971, the reserves finished second in the Combination, with 5,527 watching their game against eventual champions Spurs. In 2007 the reserves folded for three seasons due to the expense of running a side that wasn't able to be competitive.

TOP GOALSCORERS PER SEASON

Season	Player	Goals
1961/62	Bud Houghton	43
1960/61	Tony Jones	38
1984/85	John Aldridge	34
1959/60	Geoff Denial	32
1985/86	John Aldridge	31
1957/58	Jack Cross	27
1958/59	Joe Dickson	27
2008/09	James Constable	26
2009/10	James Constable	26
1954/55	Harry Yates	25
1955/56	Jimmy Smillie	25
1983/84	Steve Biggins	24
1994/95	Paul Moody	24
1995/96	Paul Moody	24
1950/51	Bill Rowstron	24
1964/65	Colin Booth	23
1996/97	Nigel Jemson	23
1958/59	Jimmy Jackson	23
1961/62	Alan Willey	23
1981/82	Keith Cassells	22
1952/53	Harry Yates	22

SWIPE ME

AFTER the Hillsborough disaster on April 15th 1989, there was a lot of demand for improved safety measures and membership schemes at football grounds. Oxford's response was to become the first club in the country to introduce the season ticket in the form of a swipe card as a means to gain entry to the ground, for the 1989/90 season. The idea was that supporters would swipe their card through a card reader at the turnstile and this would enable them to pass through, thereby obviating the need for turnstile operators. Apart from some delays with the printing of the cards, the system worked fine for the first couple of games, but the club then found that turnstile operators were needed after all. A similar system was considered for the Kassam Stadium, but the cost was found to be prohibitive.

REGISTRATION FEE

IN January 2009, Oxford United were deducted five points by the Conference board for playing midfielder Eddie Hutchinson without registering him. Hutchinson was in his third season at the club, but had been transfer-listed by Darren Patterson before the start of the season and he had spent some time on trial with Cambridge United before returning to the club. Patterson had no intention of playing Hutchinson, who was made to train with the youth team, but injuries forced his hand and he came on as a substitute on August 16th, scoring in the 6-3 win over Weymouth. Hutch started in the next four games, and also made three substitute appearances, before the error came to light. There was a possibility that United could have been deducted 11 points, the number gained in games in which Hutchinson played, but the five-point penalty reflected the games in which he started. United, who chose not to appeal, were also fined £500, with a further fine of £3,500 suspended until May 2010. At the end of the 2008/09 season, Oxford missed the play-offs by just four points.

OLD MCDONALD

THE Hutchinson saga (or Hutchgate as it was called by Oxford fans) wasn't the first time that the club had got into trouble with player registrations. In 1951, United were expelled from the FA Cup for fielding an ineligible player and, to make matters worse, it was after beating local neighbours Wycombe Wanderers, United winning 3-2 in the second qualifying round on October 13th. Headington featured future England goalkeeper Colin McDonald, who was on Burnley's books but seeing out his National Service at the army camp at Moreton-in-Marsh. Burnley had given McDonald permission to play for United, but when Headington asked for clearance to play him in the FA Cup they refused. Nevertheless, United registered McDonald as an amateur with the Oxfordshire FA and played him anyway. Wycombe filed a complaint and the matter was investigated by an FA commission. The commission determined that McDonald was played without Burnley's consent and they expelled United from that season's FA Cup competition, with Wycombe going into the next round instead, where they lost 2-1 at home to Aylesbury. United were also fined five guineas. McDonald never played for Headington again, and after returning to Turf Moor he became a resounding success, winning eight England caps.

FLYING HIGH

ALTHOUGH United's three seasons in the top flight were a struggle to avoid relegation, they did clock up some impressive results. The only teams they failed to beat were West Bromwich Albion, with whom they drew twice in 1985/86, Birmingham City, Watford, Liverpool, and Tottenham Hotspur. In fact United have never beaten Liverpool or Spurs, having drawn once in seven meetings with the Reds and three times in nine fixtures with Tottenham. Good results from the First Division days include a 5-0 win over Leicester City – which was Oxford's first and best win in the top flight – in their third game at that level. United also won 4-1 at Chelsea, beat Ipswich Town 4-3 – having been 3-0 down – beat Arsenal 3-0 to stay up in the final game of the 1985/86 season, beat Portsmouth 4-2 in the opening game two seasons later, and beat Norwich City 3-0 in United's final season of Division One football.

INTERNATIONALS XI (CAPPED WHILE AT OXFORD)

Kearns (Eire)

Slatter (Wales) Roberts (Wales) Melville (Wales) Langan (Eire)

Saunders (Wales) Houghton (Eire) Magilton (NI) Sloan (NI)

Aldridge (Eire) Charles (Wales)

PLAYING OFF

OXFORD have been eligible for the play-offs in every season since they were introduced in 1986. The first two seasons after their introduction involved teams at the bottom of Division One playing off against teams at the top of Division Two in order to decide promotion and relegation issues. In 2002 play-offs were introduced to determine promotion from the Conference to the Football League. Despite this, Oxford have only twice competed in the play-offs. They finished second in the Conference in 2007. In the first leg of the semi-final Oxford won 1-0 at Exeter City, who won the return game 2-1; United lost the resultant penalty shoot-out. In 2010, Oxford finished third in the Conference, and then beat Rushden & Diamonds 2-0 in the semi-final second leg after a 1-1 draw at Nene Park. In the final, United beat York 3-1 with goals from Matt Green, James Constable, and Alfie Potter to return to the Football League.

THE PRODIGALS RETURN

A NUMBER of players have had two spells at United, the first notable one being Hugh Curran, who Oxford signed from Wolves for £50,000 in September 1972; he spent two years at the Manor before moving to Bolton Wanderers for £40,000. Three years later he returned to Oxford for just over a season, during which he added 11 goals to the 32 he had scored first time around. He retired injured in 1979. Paul Moody's goals helped United to promotion in 1996, when he scored 24 times to add to the 24 he'd notched the previous campaign. He arrived at Oxford from Southampton in February 1994, but despite Moody's eight goals in 14 games United were relegated to Division Three. After winning promotion two seasons later, Moody's goals dried up and he contributed only seven during 1996/97 before he was sold to Fulham for £200,000. With Oxford in the bottom division and in desperate need of goals, they signed Moody from Millwall for £150,000 in September 2001. Moody scored on his debut against Southend United and ended the season as leading scorer with 11 goals before joining Aldershot.

BOBBY Ford made his United debut five months before Moody, having come through the youth ranks. After 11 goals in 149 games, Ford was sold to Sheffield United for £400,000 at a time when Oxford were struggling financially. He spent three seasons at Bramall Lane, before returning to Oxford on a free transfer in July 2002, but after one unhappy season he left for Bath City. Perhaps the most famous of United's two-timers is Joey Beauchamp, who came through the ranks, making his debut in May 1989. He played 143 games, scoring 25 goals, before sealing a £1 million move to West Ham United in May 1994. Sixteen months later, Joey returned to Oxford, via Swindon, for £75,000 and went on to play a further 285 games, scoring 52 goals, before retiring through injury in 2001. Joey was voted Oxford's Player of the Decade for the 1990s. Nigel Jemson arrived from Notts County for £60,000 in 1996 and was top scorer with 23 goals in his first season. He had added another ten goals to his account before, in January 1998, United received £100,000 for him from Bury. He returned to Oxford from Ayr United in January 2000. However, he failed to score in any of his 18 games that season and moved on to Shrewsbury Town that summer. Another returnee was defender Phil Gilchrist.

THE centre-back departed for Premiership side Leicester City for £500,000 in August 1999. Seven years later he was back in yellow, joining from Rotherham United, with the U's using a £50,000 prize from a Coca-Cola competition to pay his wages. In October 2007, he retired and went to manage at Woking. The most recent players to return are Jamie Cook and Chris Hargreaves. Cook left for Boston United, but returned when the '12th Man' initiative funded his £5,000 transfer from Crawley Town in September 2009. Hargreaves was released in May 2006, but returned in January 2010 after 2½ seasons, and one promotion, at Torquay United.

RECENT RECORDS

SINCE relegation to the Conference in 2006, United have set a number of new records. In their first season, the U's went unbeaten for their first 18 league games, setting a new club and Conference record for an unbeaten start. Also that season, the 11,065 who attended the Boxing Day game against Woking set a new Conference attendance record for a non play-off final. The following season, Oxford set a new club record by using 41 players during the campaign; these included Ryan Semple (one substitute appearance at Forest Green Rovers), goalkeeper Sam Warrell, loanee Patrick Collins, Chris Tardif, Declan Benjamin (two appearances), and Phil Gilchrist and Kieron St. Aimee (three appearances).

YOUTH IN CHARGE

WHO has won a league championship medal and been relegated in the same season? Mark Lawrenson is Oxford's youngest manager, being 31 years old when he was appointed by Kevin Maxwell on March 25th 1988, just one week after he was forced to retire from playing with Liverpool after rupturing an Achilles tendon against Wimbledon. However, he had played enough games for title-winners Liverpool to qualify for a medal. Lawrenson's first act as boss was to dismiss coach Ray Graydon, before trying unsuccessfully to bring in Frank Stapleton as his number two. Although Lawro gave the team talk before United's 0-0 draw at Charlton Athletic the following day, his first official game as manager was on Tuesday 28th March at home to Arsenal, another goalless draw. However, United won just two more points in Lawrenson's eight further games and the team was relegated from the top flight, 11 points from safety.

BOSSING THE FUTURE

WHEN Oxford, top of Division Two, beat Arsenal, top of Division One, 3-2 in the third round of the Milk Cup in October 1984, the game featured three players who would later go on to manage United. In the yellow was Malcolm Shotton, Oxford's captain, who was appointed manager in succession to Malcolm Crosby in January 1998, following a supporter-led campaign orchestrated by fan Neil Wakefield and supported by the fanzines *Rage On* and *Yellow Fever*. Shotton left by mutual consent on October 25th 1999, with the side fourth from bottom of Division Two. Arsenal's side featured Graham Rix and Brian Talbot. Rix succeeded Ian Atkins in March 2004, but only lasted until November before being relieved of his duties, to be followed by Ramon Díaz. Talbot had the unenviable task of following Díaz, taking over in May 2005. By the time he left, in March 2006, United were third from bottom of the fourth division and heading for relegation from the Football League.

OUFC ALL AMERICAS XI

	Busby Jr. (USA)		
M. Díaz (Arg)	Wilsterman (Sur)	Watson (Can)	Corbo (Uru)
E. Díaz (Arg)	Cooke (Dom)	Cominelli (Arg)	Raponi (Arg)
	Francis (SKN)	Anthrobus (Bar)	

A FLEETING GLIMPSE OF GOALS

OXFORD (née Headington) and Ebbsfleet United (née Gravesend & Northfleet) have scored an astonishing 129 goals in their 35 meetings (an average of almost 3.7 a game). The first time they played at the Manor they shared 11 goals as United won 6-5, equalling the club's highest aggregate score for a league fixture. United's worst defeat to the Fleet was 4-0 at Stonebridge Road in December 1955, whereas United have scored at least four goals against them on nine occasions. These include home wins of 8-2 and 8-0 in April and September 1961 and a 6-0 away win in February 1962. Chris Wilder's first home game in charge was a 5-1 win over Ebbsfleet. The sides have drawn 0-0 just once, on November 17th 2007 at the Kassam Stadium.

SAME NAME, DIFFERENT PERSON

IT is a weird coincidence that two of United's most successful managers have had namesakes among the club's players. Arthur Turner (the manager) came from Birmingham City to take over from Harry Thompson on New Year's Day 1959. Under his management the club rose from the Southern League to the Second Division, became the first Fourth Division side to reach the quarter-finals of the FA Cup, and achieved a level of success and professionalism previously undreamt of in the city. He was in charge for 504 games in just over ten years before being replaced by Ron Saunders and becoming general manager. Arthur Turner (the player) was an RAF officer who played part-time for Charlton Athletic, making a total of nine appearances in Charlton's run to the FA Cup final in 1946, and played at centre-forward in the final, thus becoming the only player to play in an FA Cup final who never played a league game for his club. In 1947, Turner moved to Colchester United, and scored the Essex club's first Football League goal at Layer Road. He retired from football in the summer of 1951, before returning to play for Headington in their 1952/53 double-winning season, scoring 15 goals in 22 games. Jim Smith (manager) took over from Ian Greaves in March 1982, eventually guiding United to the Third Division and Second Division championships in successive seasons, the only time this feat has been achieved. He left Oxford before he could manage them in the top flight, and was in charge of Queens Park Rangers when Oxford beat them 3-0 in the Milk Cup final in April 1986. He returned to Oxford over 20 years later, just before the U's were relegated to the Conference. Despite leading them to second in the table in 2007, the side lost in the play-off semi-finals and the following October Smith resigned to concentrate on his directorial duties, although he stood down as a director just over a year later. Jim Smith (player) joined Headington United as a 14-year old in April 1938, scoring on his debut against Osberton Radiators. He was with United until September 1955 when he was forced to retire through injury. He was the longest-serving amateur in the Southern League, playing 142 games and scoring 22 goals. He was given a testimonial in October 1956 against an All-Star XI, which featured Stanley Matthews. Over 10,000 fans turned up.

IT'S A WOMAN'S GAME

OXFORD Ladies were formed in 1991 and elected to Division One of the Southern Region League. In their first season they won the championship and lost the League Cup final in a penalty shoot-out. The following season they moved up to the National League, which is when Oxford United took them on and they changed their name to Oxford United Ladies. The Ladies finished the season in mid-table, but had a lot of success in five-a-side tournaments, winning the Southern Region tournament in 1992 and 1993, and also triumphing in tournaments in Portsmouth, Milton Keynes, Swindon, Witney, Thame, and Launton. During the 1992/93 season, several games were played at the Manor, with others at Abingdon Town. In 1993 the club had another name change, to Oxford United WFC, and they started playing their home games at Witney Town. In 1995 they finished third in the FA Women's Premier League Division One (South) and reached the semi-final of the League Cup, losing 2-1 to Wimbledon. They relocated to Abingdon in 1995. In 2001 the association with Oxford United came to an end and the side changed its name to Rover Oxford, playing in the Southern Region Premier League. Oxford United re-established Oxford United Ladies in 2005, playing at Roman Way, and in their first season they won Thames Valley Division One, the Thames Valley League Cup, and the Oxfordshire FA County Cup. They were promoted to the Southern Region Division One in 2006, which they won at the first attempt.

JUMPING JACK CAS

APART from player-coach Harry Thompson, United's first full-time professional footballer was Jack Casley, signed from Torquay United in July 1949, initially on a one-month trial, at a wage of £6 per week. Although his preferred position was as midfielder, he played his first game for Headington in goal in a 4-1 defeat at Colchester United; his versatility meant that he was often utilised as a striker, and he scored United's first Southern League hat-trick in the club's first Southern League win, 4-2 against Guildford City at the Manor. These were his only goals for the U's. He was initially released at the end of his first season, but after he offered to halve his winter wages the board relented. After retiring in 1951, he became United's chief scout, eventually stepping down in 2002, aged 75.

WIDELY KNOWN FACTS THAT ARE WORTH RESTATING ANYWAY

- When Oxford won Division Three in 1984, and Division Two the following season, they became the first team to perform this feat, which has yet to be repeated.
- United were the first Fourth Division side to reach the quarter-finals of the FA Cup when they lost 2-1 to Preston North End in 1964.
- Oxford were the first side to have won a major trophy to get relegated to the Conference.
- Oxford were elected to the Football League in 1962 after Accrington Stanley went bankrupt. When United were relegated to the Conference in 2006, they were replaced by Accrington Stanley.

SHINING LIGHT ON THE SUBJECT

THE first game that United played under floodlights was at the Manor on December 18th 1950. Original opponents Oxford City declined an invitation to play, but Banbury Spencer stepped in to play the game – with the authorisation of the Oxfordshire FA – in aid of the Wingfield-Morris Orthopaedic Hospital (now the Nuffield Orthopaedic Centre). A crowd of 2,603 saw Headington win 3-0 under lights loaned to the club by the Southern Electricity Board, on scaffold poles provided by Knowles & Son. The experiment was so successful that the club arranged further floodlit games against Swindon Town (0-0), Northampton Town (0-1), and Millwall (0-0), before the lights had to be dismantled and returned to the SEB on March 1st. Millwall were guaranteed a minimum of £150 to take part. The Swindon game was the clubs' first meeting, and the brightness of the lights was increased after concern that there were some parts of the pitch that were too dim against Banbury; this probably wasn't helped by the heavy snow, which forced the club to use a normal brown ball instead of the hoped-for white version. By way of thanks, the club donated £20 to the Southern Electricity Welfare Fund, £10 to electrician Mr A. T. Lees and his assistants, and 100 cigarettes to Mr Marshall. On March 20th the board approved the installation of permanent floodlighting equipment at an estimated cost of £250 (later doubled to £500). Headington's 4-3 win over Gravesend & Northfleet on February 28th 1952 was the first Southern League game to be played under floodlights. In 1963 the 18 floodlight poles were replaced by four pylons.

BACK FROM THE DEAD

UNITED'S most memorable comeback came on November 23rd 1985. It was Ipswich Town's first visit to the Manor, and goals from Kevin Wilson and a Mark Brennan penalty gave the visitors a 2-0 half-time lead. Jason Dozzell made the score 3-0 shortly into the second half; it signalled the start of a great turnaround. John Aldridge scored a hat-trick in ten minutes past debutant keeper Jon Hallworth to level the scores, and with ten minutes remaining Neil Slatter scored his first Oxford goal to earn the U's three precious points; Ipswich were relegated at the end of the season, one point behind Oxford. This feat was almost replicated on March 16th 1991, when United visited Molineux. Oxford found themselves 3-0 down at half-time as a Steve Bull hat-trick gave Wolves an apparently unassailable lead. However, second-half goals from Andy Melville, Paul Simpson, and substitute Mark Stein brought the scores level, and Stein also hit the crossbar in the final minute as the game ended 3-3. Twenty months later, Oxford found themselves 5-2 down at home to Portsmouth with 17 minutes remaining, but two goals in the last 90 seconds rescued an unlikely point in a 5-5 draw. Conversely, on Thursday 11th October 2007, in a game live on Setanta TV, Oxford took a 3-0 first-half lead over Torquay United, through Eddie Hutchinson and two goals from Yemi Odubade. However, Oxford threw away the lead when former Yellow Tim Sills equalised in the last minute. More disappointingly, United were 3-0 up at half-time against Swindon Town on Boxing Day 1977, but Swindon managed to scrape the draw. This was the first time that Town had come back from three down to get a point since January 14th 1899. In the Coca-Cola Cup first round, second leg, in August 1997, United took a 2-0 first-leg lead to Home Park. At half-time they were 3-0 down and looking like heading out of the cup, with Nigel Jemson and Joey Beauchamp almost coming to blows. In the second half Beauchamp started the revival with a stunning goal, which was added to by strikes from Jemson, Darren Purse, Matt Murphy, and another from Beauchamp, who was denied his only hat-trick for the club by Argyle keeper Jon Sheffield, who also produced a smart save from a Mark Angel drive as Oxford came back to win from 3-0 down, away from home, for the only time.

THE LONG AND THE SHORT OF IT

KEVIN Francis, at 6ft 7ins, is almost certainly the tallest player ever to have played for United. At the other end of the scale, Sam Deering and Vic Barney, who were both 5ft 5ins, were possibly the shortest.

TOO MANY CHIEFS

DURING Firoz Kassam's time in charge, from April 1st 1999 to March 21st 2006, Oxford had 15 managers: Malcolm Shotton, Mickey Lewis, Denis Smith, Mike Ford, David Kemp, Mike Ford (again), Mark Wright, Ian Atkins, David Oldfield, Graham Rix, Darren Patterson, Ramon Díaz, David Oldfield, Brian Talbot and Darren Patterson. He also employed two directors of football; Ray Harford and Joe Kinnear.

BREVITY: WIT'S SOUL

THE first managerial reign of David Oldfield was undoubtedly the shortest of any manager. After Ian Atkins was placed on gardening leave, Oldfield took charge for the game at Mansfield Town on March 20th 2004, but with the game goalless it was abandoned at half-time due to high winds. Graham Rix was appointed before United's next game, at home to Doncaster Rovers. Oldfield's second spell in charge didn't last much longer, as he took control of the last game of the 2004/05 season, a 1-0 defeat at home to Chester City, between the departure of Ramon Díaz and the arrival of Brian Talbot.

SOCIOLOGICALLY SPEAKING

UNITED are (probably) unique in having two eminent sociologists on the board simultaneously. Desmond Morris was vice-chair, having been co-opted onto the board in 1977. A year later Morris invited chartered psychologist Peter Marsh to join the board. Both used the opportunity to study the behaviour of Oxford fans for publication, with Morris's *The Soccer Tribe* published in 1981 and Marsh contributing to *The Rules of Disorder* in 1978. Morris also designed the current club badge. Marsh resigned three weeks after Robert Maxwell took over, and later became spokesman for the Save Oxford Soccer campaign to prevent the proposed merger with Reading. Morris stood down in March 1983.

LONG BARROW

BARROW have something of a special relationship with Oxford. They were United's first opponents in the Football League, on August 18th 1962, when Barrow won 3-2; Oxford's record Football League win of 7-0 was against them in Division Four, on December 19th 1964. Barrow's first game back in the Conference, after relegation in 1986, was at home to Oxford, on August 8th 2008, the Bluebirds winning 3-0 live on Setanta TV. The sides have met 14 times, 12 in the league; neither side has won away from home.

NOT AT THE RACES

WHILE United's record at Holker Street is poor, their record at Wrexham's Racecourse Ground was even worse. Before winning 1-0 there on September 12th 2009, the U's had visited Wrexham 11 times without winning, including a 1-1 draw in April 2006, the last away game before relegation to the Conference.

HATFUL OF GOALS

IN the 33 games that they have played against each other, Oxford and Luton Town have managed to score 110 goals, an average of 3.3 (recurring) a game. In their first meeting, on September 1st 1970, Luton won 4-0 at Kenilworth Road, while the two First Division meetings in 1987/88 produced 18 goals, the Hatters winning 5-2 at the Manor and then, in an extraordinary game, 7-4 in Luton. The previous season United did the double over Luton, winning 4-2 at home and 3-2 away. The only times the sides have shared a goalless draw was in October 2000, at the Manor.

THE EMPIRE STRIKES BACK

TWO people involved with Oxford have been awarded an MBE. Steve Perryman received his medal in 1984 for services to football while at Tottenham Hotspur. He moved to Oxford in 1986, making 17 appearances before going to Brentford. Goalkeeping coach Alan Hodgkinson received his award, also for services to football, in the 2008 New Year's Honours List. He had played 576 league games for Sheffield United and won five England caps, and coached for Manchester United, Rangers, and Scotland before joining United in July 2005.

JUVE GOT TO BE KIDDING

IN February 1997, the news broke that Oxford United chairman Robin Herd was holding talks with officials from Italian giants Juventus about a formal link between the two clubs. The common connection was Formula One, with Herd being the former owner of the March racing team, and Ferrari belonging to the Agnelli family, who also owned Juventus. At the same time there were strong rumours circulating that Benetton, owned by Flavio Briatore and Oxford fan Eddie Jordan, were also involved. Two directors from Juventus visited the Manor on February 2nd to watch United's 4-1 defeat by Manchester City and hold informal talks, while Juventus general manager Luciano Moggi, executive vice-president Roberto Bettega, and director Antonio Giraudo attended the 3-1 win over Oldham Athletic two weeks later, after visiting Briatore at Benetton's HQ near Witney. However, a Juventus spokesman dismissed the idea of Oxford taking on Juve youngsters and providing coaching as "wild imagination", while Briatore himself claimed that the reports of him buying out Oxford and investing £10 million in the team were "pure fantasy". Nevertheless, United went as far as commissioning an away strip in Juventus's colours of black and white stripes, although it was never used except as fans' team Raging Fever's second kit.

FIRSTS AMONG EQUALS

THERE are many firsts connected with Oxford: Alex Ferguson's first game as Manchester United manager was a 2-0 defeat at the Manor on November 8th 1986; Mark Hughes also made his Manchester United debut against Oxford, scoring as the sides drew 1-1 in the Milk Cup fourth round at the Manor on November 30th 1983; Jose Mourinho's first game as Chelsea manager was a pre-season friendly at the Kassam Stadium on July 17th 2004, the game ending 1-1; Paul Gascoigne scored his first career goal, for Newcastle United, in a 3-0 defeat at St. James' Park on September 21st 1985, while Osvaldo Ardiles' first home game as manager of Newcastle was a 2-2 draw with Oxford on April 10th 1991; the first game for Birmingham City after Ian Sullivan and Karen Brady took control was a 1-0 home defeat by United on March 6th 1993; Trevor Francis, England's first £1 million transfer, made his Birmingham debut aged just 16, scoring in a 1-1 draw against Oxford at St. Andrew's on September 12th 1970.

THE HARDER THEY COME

WHILE Oxford have yet to win at Old Trafford, Anfield, White Hart Lane, or Highbury (they have yet to play at the Emirates), on the flip side United have never lost at home to Arsenal, Everton, or Stoke City. Of the top clubs, it is only Liverpool and Spurs who remain unbeaten by the U's.

GOING TO THE WALL

IN the 28 games between Oxford and Walsall, the sides have shared 95 goals, of which 63 have been scored by United. The first two times that Walsall visited the Manor they conceded 13 goals; they were beaten 6-1 in a League Cup first round replay on September 7th 1964, and 7-1 in a Division Three match on December 27th 1965. In the League Cup game, Bill Calder scored four goals, while Graham Atkinson bagged a hat-trick in the league match. United also beat Walsall 4-0 in 1967, 4-2 in 1982, 6-3 in 1983, and 5-1 at Fellows Park in 1988. In that last game, four of United's goals were scored by Richard Hill, the first United player to hit four away from home since January 1949, when Ray Mansell scored five at Amersham in the Spartan League. The Saddlers have only twice scored as many as three goals against Oxford, first in that 6-3 defeat and more recently when they won 3-2 at the Bescot in August 2000.

SPREADING THE LIGHT

SOME supporters can be just a bit too helpful. In 1996/97 Oxford were drawn away to Watford in the FA Cup third round, to be played on January 4th. The game was postponed because of a frozen pitch and rescheduled for January 14th, but five minutes before kick-off the referee deemed that the pitch was still too frozen and the game was again postponed. On January 21st the rescheduled match was due to start when the floodlights failed. With the game about to be called off for the third time, an Oxford-supporting electrician volunteered to have a look at the problem and eventually managed to get the lights working. Ninety minutes later he was probably regretting his intervention, as Watford won 2-0 to eliminate United from the cup.

FESTIVE SPIRIT

THE Festival of Britain was a national festival that was opened on May 3rd 1951. Oxford was chosen as one of the centres where major festivities were to take place, and Headington United got on board with the festive spirit by playing two friendly games. On April 16th the club entertained Scottish side St. Johnstone in a game billed as a Festival of Britain Challenge, even though it took place over a fortnight before the Festival was due to start. Headington were in festive mood, beating the Saints 7-0, with Bill Rowstron and Jim Smith both scoring hat-tricks and Vic Barney scoring the other goal. A second Festival of Britain game took place on May 14th at the University Sports Ground on Iffley Road. Over 10,000 spectators saw Headington draw 1-1 with Belgian side Royal Ixelles, with Jim Smith again on the scoresheet for United.

TOP 20 GOALSCORERS

Graham Atkinson	107 goals
Tony Jones	100 goals
John Aldridge	90 goals
Peter Foley	90 goals
Joey Beauchamp	77 goals
Bud Houghton	75 goals
Paul Moody	75 goals
Billy Rees	60 goals
Matt Murphy	55 goals
Harry Yates	54 goals
James Constable	52 goals
Geoff Denial	51 goals
Paul Simpson	50 goals
Steve Basham	49 goals
Alan Willey	48 goals
John Durnin	47 goals
John Shuker	47 goals
Johnny Love	45 goals
Andy Thomas	45 goals
Martin Foyle	44 goals

EVERYONE'S AWAY

THE largest away crowd to visit the Kassam Stadium since it was finished in 2001 is the 4,603 that Leyton Orient brought with them for the final game of the 2005/06 season. Orient needed a win to ensure automatic promotion from the bottom tier, while Oxford needed the three points to avoid relegation to the Conference. Needless to say, it was the away support that went home happy. The Orient supporters comprised 37.6 per cent of the attendance, a ground record 12,243. The second largest away crowd for a league game is the 2,788 who followed Bristol Rovers on April 21st 2003, which was 31.9 per cent of the 8,732 in attendance. They also went home happy after their 1-0 win ensured that they were safe from relegation to the Conference. In the same period, the best attendance to follow Oxford on the road was the 2,333 who went to Rushden & Diamonds on April 29th 2010, comprising 51 per cent of the 4,537 gate. Conversely, the lowest away crowd to grace the Kassam for a league fixture is the 29 Histon followers who made the trip on February 13th 2010 to watch their team lose 2-0. That equates to 0.5 per cent of the total attendance of 5,365, and is slightly lower than the 39 that Farsley Celtic brought with them in April 2008. The smallest following that Oxford have taken with them in the same period is 147, who visited Rochdale on Tuesday 27th September 2005 to witness a rare Barry Quinn goal earn United the points.

THE EXORCIST

AT the start of November 2001 the Bishop of Oxford performed a ceremony at the newly built Kassam Stadium. Les Wells, who originally owned the land, allowed gypsies to stay in return for helping him with harvesting and hay-making, but when the field was sold to the club, the gypsies were evicted and allegedly cast a curse. This was blamed for the club's poor start to their first campaign in the new ground, and the ceremony was performed as a blessing to remove the curse. However, the Right Reverend Richard Harries said the curse was not the reason for the visit. Instead, he used a prayer which said; "Bless this place and protect it from evil." Several players joined the bishop and the club chairman, Firoz Kassam, for the blessing.

SIMPLE MAJORITY

SINCE relegation to the Conference, Oxford supporters comprised more than half the attendance at 13 away games. The first time was at Forest Green Rovers' New Lawn, where 1,640 of the 3,027 crowd were in the away terrace. This was a Friday evening game on October 6th 2006, and every time United have played at Forest Green in a Conference fixture there have been more U's fans than home supporters. At St. Albans later that season, United had 68.2 per cent of the crowd, their highest percentage, with 1,168 in the Clarence Park away end.

ROYALISTS V ROUNDHEADS

ON April 16th 1983, after Oxford won 1-0 at Doncaster Rovers, the news broke that chairman Robert Maxwell intended to merge United with Reading and form a new club to be called Thames Valley Royals, to play at an unspecified site. The scheme had the support of Reading's chairman Frank Waller, the Football League, and the *Oxford Mail*, although it was met with a hostile reception by both sets of supporters. The Oxford board knew nothing of the proposal before the announcement, but they too gave it their support, on the condition that the club be called Thames Valley United instead. The mayor of Didcot recommended that the club should relocate there, to the dismay of the local populace, who were fearful of hooliganism. United supporters formed SOS (Save Oxford Soccer) and staged a peaceful pitch invasion before their home game against Wigan Athletic on April 23rd. United's home game against Reading on May 2nd had its kick-off moved to 11am, and United supporters held a protest march from Oxford bus station to the Manor. Maxwell confronted the protestors at Gloucester Green, but he was shouted down. Former director Peter Marsh called on Oxford City Council to take a controlling share in the club, as a valuable community resource, to no avail. However, it was at the Reading end that the proposal was eventually scuppered after opponents to the merger forced an injunction on Waller preventing him from selling his shares to Maxwell. This was extended into the summer, meaning that both clubs had to plan for the next season as separate entities. In May, Waller was forced to resign by former player Roger Smee, killing the idea. Maxwell, who had threatened to quit if the merger failed, remained Oxford's chairman.

BRISTOL FASHION

DENIS Smith succeeded Brian Horton as manager of Oxford in September 1993, after leaving Bristol City, and his first game in charge was against his former teammates at the Manor on September 11th. Oxford won a bad-tempered game 4-2, which ended with Smith and City manager Russell Osman, Smith's former player-coach at Ashton Gate, having a confrontation in the tunnel after Smith accused Osman of provoking David Penney into getting sent off. Smith's links with Bristol City weren't finished, though. In his second spell as Oxford manager, his first game in charge was again against the Robins, with City winning 1-0 at the Manor on February 5th 2000, and his final game as United boss was also against Bristol City, on September 30th 2002, another 1-0 home defeat. After this game, with United rooted to the foot of the Second Division, Smith resigned.

THE WALL CAME TUMBLING DOWN

AT Oxford's home FA Cup fourth round tie against Watford on January 23rd 1971, a goalmouth scramble at the London Road end of the ground, with Oxford on the attack, caused a surge of spectators in the packed terrace, resulting in the wall at the foot of the stand collapsing and part of the crowd spilling onto the pitch. The referee had to take the players off for several minutes while the police and St. John's Ambulance tended to those injured. Seven people had to be taken to hospital, although none were detained. Six of the injured boys were Oxford supporters, and they were invited to attend United's next home game, against Sheffield United, as guests of the club. The other injury, a Watford-supporting youth, was invited by Watford to attend the fourth round replay, the first game having ended in a 1-1 draw once play had resumed, with the Hornets scoring a very late equaliser. The attendance at the game was 17,814, and United won the replay 2-1 to set up a fifth round tie against Leicester City. This is the only known instance of such infrastructure damage at the Manor, and it came just three weeks after the Ibrox disaster, in which 66 people lost their lives. United later agreed to pay half the cost of replacing the permanent advertising hoarding that was destroyed in the collapse, at a cost to the club of £12.50.

SAME NAME, SAME GAME

WHEN Matt Green came on as a second-half substitute in Oxford's FA Trophy first round tie against Hayes & Yeading on December 12th 2009, he joined Franny Green, who was in the starting line-up. They became the first unrelated players with the same surname to play together since Luke and Martin Foster, whose last game together was on April 21st 2007. Mike and Bobby Ford last played together on November 22nd 1997 at Norwich City, while Derek and Colin Clarke last appeared in the same game on August 17th 1976 in the League Cup at Cambridge. On November 6th 1954, Jim and Ken Smith played their last game together in a 1-0 FA Cup win over Tonbridge. In 1956/57, Don and Eddie Adams featured, but none of Don's six games coincided with Eddie's 31 appearances.

SCORES ON THE DOORS

UNITED'S best win in the Southern League was 9-0 versus Wisbech on December 10th 1960. Their best win in the Football League was 7-0 against Barrow on December 19th 1964.

HOME BREAKDOWN

IN 1980/81 Oxford did not win a Third Division home game until November 15th, when they beat Chester City 1-0, by which time they were in 21st place. The win over Chester was watched by 2,526; United's lowest home crowd for a Football League game. This could have been worse but for their away form, with four wins on the road including a 4-0 win at Fulham's Craven Cottage. In their ten home games, United had drawn four and lost six, although they had beaten both Southend United and Chesterfield at the Manor in the League Cup.

FORTRESS MANOR

BETWEEN August 11th 1979, when they were beaten 5-1 by Reading, and September 28th 1988, when Bristol City won 4-2, United played 27 League Cup games at the Manor without defeat. Included in that run were wins over Newcastle United, Leeds United, and Manchester United (1983), Arsenal (1984), Aston Villa (1986), and Manchester United (1988).

MASTERS OF THE UNIVERSE

DURING the Glory Years of the mid-1980s, it wasn't just proper football at which United excelled; they weren't bad at the small-sided game either. In November 1985 Oxford won the *Daily Express* National Five-a-Side Championship at Wembley Arena. After beating Watford 1-0, West Ham United 2-1, and Nottingham Forest 3-1, United then beat Arsenal 1-0 in a sudden-death penalty shoot-out after drawing 2-2. The hero for Oxford was goalkeeper Paul Whittington, on loan from Oxford City. Earlier in the day he had played for United's reserves in their 1-0 defeat by QPR, Gary Cooper scoring with a penalty. In the championship final he saved a penalty from Ian Allinson to win the trophy in front of a capacity 8,000 crowd. United defended their trophy on November 26th 1986, but after beating Aston Villa 2-0 in the first round they were beaten 1-0 by Southampton in the second round, a goal from former Manor trialist Matt le Tissier knocking out the holders in front of around 1,000 United fans, the largest contingent at the Arena. United again borrowed a goalkeeper from Oxford City, this time Paul Richardson playing for the Us, whose defence of the trophy lasted just 16 minutes. The following month, on December 10th, United featured in the Guinness Soccer Sixes at the Manchester G-Mex, and the U's again beat Arsenal in the final. Oxford beat Manchester United 2-1 and drew 1-1 with Chelsea before beating Aston Villa in the semi-final. They then beat Arsenal 2-1 with two goals in the final two minutes from John Aldridge and first-year professional Paul Swannack (with only 12 seconds left on the clock) in front of a capacity 5,500 crowd. Goalkeeper Steve Hardwick was voted Player of the Tournament. The following season Oxford unsuccessfully tried to defend their trophy on December 7th 1987 at the G-Mex Centre. They were drawn in Group A, but they fell at the first hurdle. A goalless draw with Newcastle United was followed by a 4-0 defeat, the biggest scoreline of the day, to Watford. United goalkeeper Peter Hucker had a nightmare, gifting Watford their first two goals. United's only consolation was the £6,000 appearance money they received. In the other group game, Watford and Newcastle drew 2-2, so Watford qualified as group winners. United had previously appeared in the *Daily Express* Five-a-Side Championship, taking part in the Southern Region Qualifying Tournament at Bracknell on May 6th 1969. After beating Brighton & Hove Albion 3-1 in the first round, they were eliminated by Gillingham, who won 3-2.

SEVENTH HEAVEN

ON October 3rd 1959, Geoff Denial scored as Headington drew 1-1 at Worcester City. He also scored the following week in a 1-0 win at Poole, and the week after as United beat King's Lynn 3-2. He then scored a week later in a 4-2 win at Yeovil and then hit a hat-trick in a 3-2 FA Cup fourth qualifying round win at Cambridge City. He was on target again the following week as United lost 2-1 at Tonbridge, and a week later he scored a penalty in a 4-3 FA Cup first round defeat at Enfield. That was the end of Denial's run, having scored in a club-record seven games in a row.

PAPER TALK

UNITED'S relations with the media haven't always been cordial. In May 2003, *Oxford Mail* reporter Jon Murray was banned from the stadium by chairman Firoz Kassam for having the temerity to report that David Savage hadn't been offered a new contract, although the ban was rescinded on July 1st. In August 1975, the *Daily Express* was censured by the Press Council for failure to correct and apologise for an erroneous statement about United in an article published earlier in the year. The story claimed that the FA was about to instigate an inquiry into the club's affairs, but chairman Tony Rosser found this to be untrue and he requested a retraction and an apology. When neither were forthcoming, he took the case to the Press Council, which found in the club's favour. In October 1974 the board banned Radio Oxford from live coverage of games as an experiment to see if crowds would increase, which they did. The club eventually backed down when other reporters threatened to boycott games in support of the BBC. In March 1951, the club held a meeting with the sports editor of the *Oxford Mail* to complain about the negative coverage they were receiving, while a year earlier the board decided against supplying the paper with the official gate figures each week. When United took the decision in 1949 to turn professional, the *Oxford Times* published a number of articles arguing against the decision, one claiming that "it cannot be said that the game in this city will be improved by Headington's decision to go over to professionalism".

WHAT MIGHT HAVE BEEN

EVERYBODY knows that Oxford beat Queens Park Rangers 3-0 in the Milk Cup final on Sunday 20th April 1986. However, if the game had ended in a draw, as unlikely as that seems in retrospect, plans had already been made by the Football League for a replay. The match would have taken place at White Hart Lane, home of Tottenham Hotspur, on Wednesday 30th April 1986, with a 7.45 kick off. Tickets for the replay had already been printed before the final, ready to go on sale immediately after the original game, if necessary.

20 LOWEST HOME ATTENDANCES

Oxford United have never had an attendance for a senior match below one thousand, but the smallest crowd of just 1,055 for a tie in the Full Members Trophy (then sponsored by Zenith Data Systems), against Portsmouth in 1990, came perilously close to three figures.

1,055..12/12/1990..Portsmouth ....1-0 .... ZDS Trophy
1,214..07/12/1999..Luton Town ....2-0 ..... Auto W/screens
1,323..21/11/1990..Bristol City ....2-2 .... ZDS Trophy
1,478..11/11/1987..Crystal Palace.............1-0 .... Simod Cup
1,508..15/12/2007..Tonbridge....................0-0 ....FA Trophy
1,518..27/09/1994..Bristol Rovers.............2-2 ..... Auto W/screens
1,521..23/11/2005..Leyton Orient............1-0 ....LDV Vans
1,560..23/11/1988..Ipswich Town..............2-3 .... Simod Cup
1,581..19/01/2010..Woking ....1-0 ....FA Trophy
1,663..12/12/2009..Hayes & Yeading Utd 1-0 ....FA Trophy
1,754..08/11/1989..Luton Town ....2-3 .... ZDS Trophy
1,797..11/01/2000..Wycombe Wdrs..........1-1 ..... Auto W/screens
1,842..29/09/2004..Exeter City.................2-2 ....LDV Vans
1,910..18/09/1985..Shrewsbury Town ......3-0 .....Full Memb Cup
1,936..15/08/1981..Aldershot ....0-1 .. Ftb Lge Grp Cup
1,943..28/11/1995..Colchester Utd...........1-2 ..... Auto W/screens
1,958..13/01/2009..York City....................1-2 ....FA Trophy
2,000..15/12/1949..Dartford ....1-1 ....Southern League
2,194..09/01/2007..Lewes FC....................1-0 ....FA Trophy
2,309..10/01/1995..Swansea City..............1-2 ..... Auto W/screens

A YEAR TO REMEMBER

BOTH Bud Houghton and John Aldridge have scored 34 goals in a calendar year. Houghton's came in 1962, when he scored 21 in the Southern League Premier, 11 in Division Four of the Football League, and two in the FA Cup. Houghton's league goals included a brace in United's 6-2 win over Hartlepools United, the only time that he scored more than one goal for Oxford in a Football League match. John Aldridge's year was 1986, with 25 goals in Division One, one in the FA Cup, and eight in the League Cup, coming on top of the 30 he'd scored in 1985. In 2009 James Constable scored 33 goals, of which one was in the FA Trophy, one in the FA Cup, and the remainder in the Football Conference.

DARLING BUD

BRIAN 'Bud' Houghton was an extraordinary goalscorer, hitting the net 75 times in his 114 games for United. In addition, the Madras-born striker set two goalscoring records for the club, both in the side's final Southern League season, 1961/62. He scored in 12 consecutive home games, starting on October 21st with a hat-trick in the FA Cup fourth qualifying round 3-2 win over Salisbury City. He scored 19 goals in those dozen matches. He also scored three goals in other home games to set a club record of scoring 22 home goals in a season.

IN DENIAL

GEOFF Denial was another record-breaking goalscorer to play for the club in the early 1960s. In 1959/60 he broke the club's then goalscoring record of 27 goals in a season (set two seasons earlier by Jack Cross, and equalled the next season by Joe Dickson) by scoring 32 goals. In the course of the season, Denial set the record for scoring in consecutive away games, finding the net in nine consecutive away matches, starting on September 16th in a 2-1 win at Wisbech. The run included a hat-trick in a 3-2 FA Cup fourth qualifying round win at Cambridge City. Denial played a total of 199 games for United, of which just seven occurred after election to the Football League. He scored 51 goals, but none in the league.

THE BEAUTY WITHIN

THE very first Miss Oxford United was 19-year-old Liz Andruszko, a first-year student at Westminster College. She gained her title in March 1975. Miss Andruszko, however, failed to make the top three in the Midland area 'Miss Football Queen' that year.

FROZEN OUT

UNITED'S first season as a Football League club, 1962/63, was interrupted by one of the worst winters on record. It resulted in Oxford having a record 12 games postponed, from their Boxing Day visit to Tranmere Rovers, to the March 2nd game at home to Crewe Alexandra. The only match that United were able to play in those two months was their FA Cup third round tie at Arsenal, which itself was postponed twice, eventually taking place on January 30th with the Gunners winning 5-1 on a snow-covered Highbury. The game was played at 3pm on a Wednesday afternoon, meaning that a crowd of just 14,624 was in attendance, including some 3,200 supporting United.

COOL IN THE HOT SEAT

OXFORD player-coach David Oldfield had mixed emotions in his first game in temporary charge for the clash at Mansfield on March 20th 2004, as strong winds caused the game to be abandoned for safety reasons at half -time. He took charge in the period after Ian Atkins was suspended, after agreeing to manage Bristol Rovers, and before Graham Rix arrived. United's other brief managerial encounters are:

David Oldfield	(half a game, abandoned)	– 20/03/04
David Oldfield	(one game)	– 07/05/05
Mike Ford	(two games)..................	– 01/05/01 – 05/05/01
Maurice Evans	(two games)..................	– 28/08/93 – 04/09/93
Darren Patterson ...	(three games)................	– 15/03/06 – 21/03/06
Darren Patterson ...	(three games)................	– 20/11/04 – 08/12/04
Jim Smith	(four games)	– 04/12/08 – 20/12/08
Malcolm Crosby	(five games)	– 26/12/97 – 17/01/98
Mike Ford	(six games)	– 08/10/00 – 28/10/00
Roy Barry	(seven games)...............	– 03/02/82 – 27/02/82

BUBBLING BROOKS

JAMIE Brooks must be one of the unluckiest players to have pulled on the Yellow shirt in recent years. At the end of the 2001/02 season, Brooks completed a clean sweep of all the various player of the season awards, winning the Players' Player of the Season, the Supporters' Player of the Season, the Young Player of the Season, and the Media Writers' Player of the Season awards. He was linked with a million pound move to Arsenal, and was on the verge of becoming a true U's superstar, when he was cruelly struck down with Guillain-Barré syndrome, a rare virus affecting the peripheral nervous system, which left the Oxford-born forward virtually paralysed and unable to breathe independently for several weeks. Jamie went from 11 to eight stone in just three months, while in intensive care, where he was visited by Markus Babbel, the former Germany and Liverpool defender, who had also contracted the disease, losing a year from his career. Jamie played his first game on October 8th 2000, coming on as a substitute for Paul Tait in Oxford's 2-1 defeat at Swindon Town. David Kemp gave Brooks his first start in his last match as manager, a 3-1 home win over Swansea City, in which Brooks scored his first goal. He played 31 games, scoring 11 goals, including Oxford's first competitive goal at the Kassam Stadium, before his illness. To aid his recuperation, Brooks had loan spells at Maidenhead United and Tamworth, making his first Oxford appearance after his illness in the pre-season friendly against Spurs in 2003. He wasn`t ready to resume first-team duties for over another year when, after a few brief substitute appearances, Ramon Díaz started him against Cambridge in his first game in charge. Brooks was in and out of the side for the next few months, playing another 22 games and scoring twice, but he failed to secure a regular first-team place, never recovering his pace or stamina, despite further loan spells at Slough Town and Brackley Town. His last game for United was when he came on for Lee Mansell in the club's last Football League match, against Orient. He was eventually released at the start of the 2006 season and signed for Didcot Town, turning down an offer from Grimsby Town so that he could remain in the locale. He eventually joined Oxford City in September 2008 from Abingdon Town, having also had a brief spell as a coach with the United Centre of Excellence.

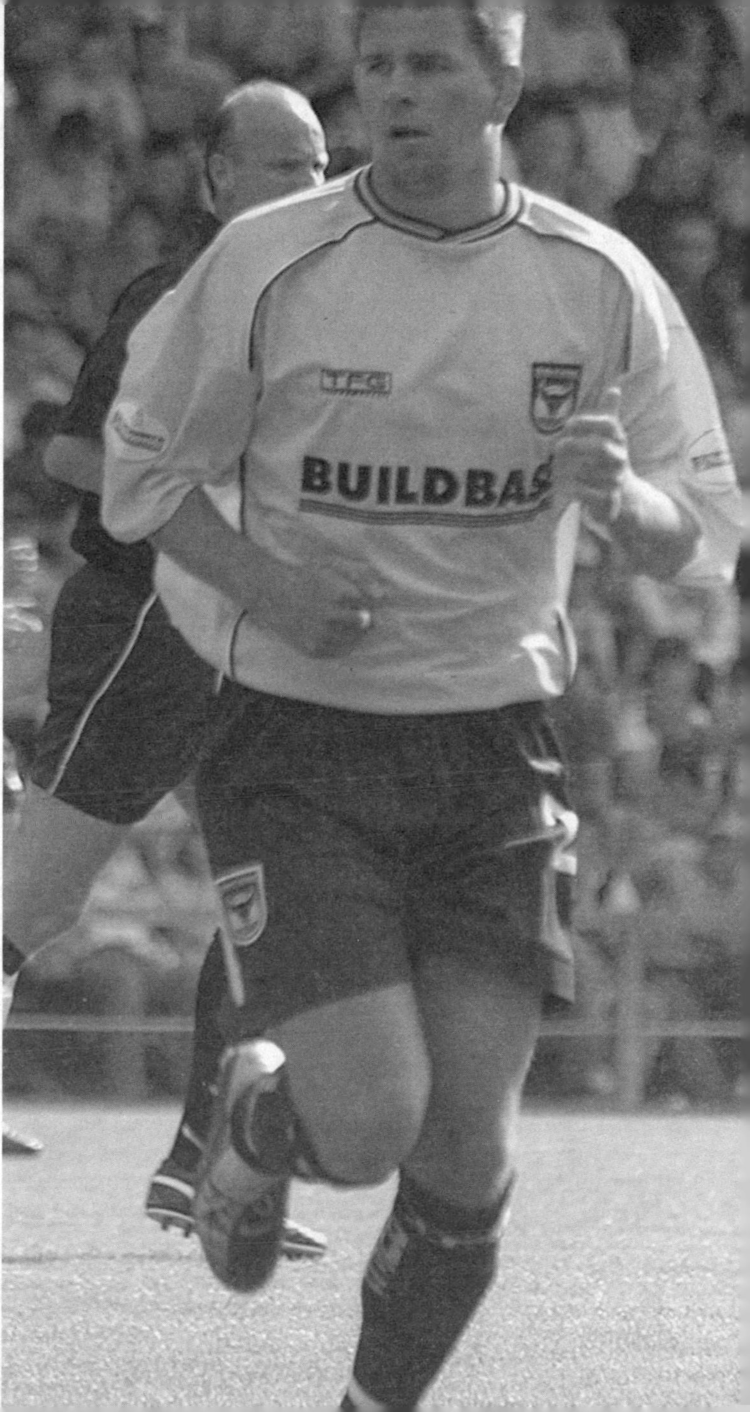

ILLNESS ROBBED JAMIE BROOKS OF POTENTIAL SUPERSTARDOM

YELLOWS FOREVER!

THE first record of the club's colours is in the minutes of the third annual meeting, on September 25th 1895, when it was confirmed that the club would play in 'Orange and Dark Blue'. These were the colours the club used, either with plain, striped, or halved shirts, for the next 64 years, although they did get into trouble with the Oxfordshire FA in 1906/07 for turning up to games in 'a medley of hues'. In 1960 the club changed its official colours to old gold (a slightly yellower version of orange) and black, coinciding with the name change to Oxford United. Despite a suggestion by Gerry Summers in April 1970 to change to a brighter all-yellow strip, these were the colours the club wore until 1973, when they finally adopted Summers' idea. They wore all-yellow for two seasons before adopting a wide-striped shirt of yellow and royal blue, with blue shorts. In 1977 the club reverted to plain shirts, dropping the blue stripes but retaining the blue shorts. This combination lasted until 1985, when promotion to the top flight was marked by a change to yellow and blue, although the current combination has seen a return to broad stripes.

STRIPPING AWAY

THE first recorded change strip comes from United's floodlit encounter with Banbury Spencer in December 1950, when the players wore white shirts and blue shorts to avoid clashing with the visitors' gold and red strip. United usually wore white shorts when there was a clash. After election to the Football League the club's away colours were all red, although they reverted to white again the following season. The change shirts alternated between red and white over the next few seasons, although in 1973 the white had a bizarre red diagonal slash across the shirt (with blue shorts). Then an odd deckchair-style red, white, and blue concoction in 1993, followed by red and black stripes from 1994 to 1997 (with an interruption in 1995 for a silvery-grey thing), after which white was again used. In 1999 the club had two seasons using a blue top with white sleeves, going back to all-white again until 2002, when navy blue was worn. In 2004 the change strip was black, but in the Conference this was prohibited and white again became the alternative, with a couple of seasons of blue in 2007 and 2008. Light blue was used for the first time in 2010.

MANOR WOMAN

THE original Manorettes were a group of 35 young girls, selected from 65 applicants, with two matrons in charge. They were kitted out in skirts and blazers in club colours of gold and black, and sold programmes and jackpot tickets around the Manor. They were the brainchild of club secretary Vic Couling and general manager Arthur Turner, and the supporters' club donated £500 towards the cost of their uniforms. The initiative was short-lived, however, as the rise in football violence meant that the girls patrolling the terraces were vulnerable, and the scheme was abandoned before the end of the first season, despite the expenditure on PVC macs. After the club moved to the Kassam Stadium the name of the Manorettes was resurrected, but this time it was for a troupe of dancing girls who entertained the supporters before games and at half-time. The girls, all aged between 12 and 16, made their debut before the visit of Bristol Rovers on February 2nd 2002 and, although the experiment was longer-lived than its predecessor, within a couple of seasons of cold winters and wet pitches the girls obviously thought of better things to be doing with their Saturday afternoons.

CHELSEA PENSIONED

WHEN Oxford visited Stamford Bridge for a top-flight match on February 8th 1986 a home win looked a formality. United had slipped into the bottom three following five successive league defeats and were without an away win in the league, while a win for Chelsea, who were unbeaten in their last 12 games, of which they had won nine, would take them to the top of the First Division for the first time in over 20 years. The winter was just starting to bite (Oxford's next two games would both be postponed because of the weather) and the Chelsea groundstaff worked beyond the call of duty to clear the pitch of snow and get the game to go ahead. Their efforts were rewarded as 16,182 witnessed Oxford's best away win in their three seasons in the top flight, as goals from John Aldridge, Jeremy Charles, Trevor Hebberd, and Chelsea old-boy Peter Rhoades-Brown earned the U's a 4-1 victory to complete the double over the Pensioners, with John Bumstead scoring Chelsea's goal. The result lifted United to 18th place and left Chelsea third, two points behind leaders Everton.

BURTON TAILORED FOR GOAL

ROY Burton is possibly United's most enigmatic goalkeeper, remembered as much for his character quirks as for his superlative shot stopping. He is also the club's longest-serving goalkeeper, having worn the gloves from when he displaced Ireland international goalie Mick Kearns in November 1971 until his final game against Newport in December 1982, after which he lost his place to John Butcher. In his 11 years between the posts, Burtie (first name Royston) played 449 games for the U's, keeping an incredible 132 clean sheets. Burton wasn't the tallest of keepers, being a shade over 5ft 9ins. tall, but some of his reflex saves will be long remembered, as will his Mexican-bandit style moustache and the unfortunate habit of his shorts revealing his derriere. Indeed, on one occasion against Crystal Palace (Peter Houseman's last game before he died) the elastic in Burton's shorts went entirely and he gave the fans in the London Road terrace an unforgettable view. John Milkins' arrival in 1974 saw Burton lose his first-team place for much of 1974/75 and part of the following season, but the aging ex-Portsmouth custodian never really convinced and it was no surprise when Burton regained his rightful spot between the sticks. After losing his place to Butcher, coupled with the arrival of Steve Hardwick from Newcastle United, Burton was released at the end of the 1982/83 season and he went on to play for Witney Town.

YET TO MEET (OR BEAT)

OF the current Football League sides, Oxford had never played against Accrington Stanley until the 2010/11 season. The original Stanley resigned from the Football League in March 1962, with United elected in their place. When Oxford were relegated to the Conference, Accrington, formed in 1970 to replace the original club, were one of the promoted sides. The other league side that United have never met is MK Dons, formed in 2004 and taking the place of Wimbledon in League One. Football League clubs that Oxford have played, but not in the league before 2010, are Dagenham, Morecambe (who won promotion in 2007), and Burton Albion, who went up in 2009. The only Football League side (apart from Liverpool and Tottenham) that Oxford have not beaten in a league match before 2010 is Aldershot; Oxford's four wins against the Shots coming in the FA Cup (twice), the Football League Trophy, and the Conference.

FIRING BLANKS

UNITED have thrice gone six games without scoring, their worst run. The first sequence started in March 1988 with goalless draws at Charlton Athletic, which was Maurice Evans' last game in charge, and at home to Arsenal, which was Mark Lawrenson's first game as manager. A 1-0 defeat at Coventry City was followed by a 0-0 draw with Southampton, and then two 3-0 defeats at Watford and against Sheffield Wednesday. A 1-1 draw with Everton finally ended the run. The second run was in October 1996, when they started the month with a goalless draw at Tranmere Rovers. A 1-0 home defeat by Swindon Town was followed by three consecutive 0-0 draws: at Barnsley, at home to Birmingham City, and then at Port Vale in the Coca-Cola Cup third round. The sequence was completed with a 2-0 defeat at Charlton, but United didn't have a completely blank month, as they broke their duck in fine style with a 4-1 win over Stoke City on October 29th. The final occasion that they failed to score in six successive games was in December 2007. The month started with a 0-0 draw against Southend United in the FA Cup second round. The following week Oxford lost 1-0 at Northwich Victoria before Southend beat the U's 3-0 in the replay. That was followed by a goalless draw at home to Tonbridge Angels in the FA Trophy second round, who then won the replay 1-0. A 1-0 defeat at Aldershot in the Setanta Shield completed the run, which was ended with a 1-0 Conference win over Crawley Town. There have also been three occasions that the club has had five consecutive games without scoring: in September/October 1968, in February/March 1971, and in January/February 2000.

DOING THE DOUBLE DOUBLE

PETERBOROUGH United were certainly sick of the sight of Oxford during the 1994/95 season. In the course of that campaign the sides met four times, twice in the league and twice in the League Cup first round, with United winning on every occasion. In the first leg of the League Cup game, Oxford won 3-1 at the Manor, and the following week they beat the Posh 1-0 at London Road. United then won at Peterborough 4-1 on Boxing Day to lead the division, and completed the league double with a 1-0 win at the Manor on April 17th 1995.

MAJORLY SECRET

UNITED have had their fare share of interesting characters in charge of the club – most notably Robert Maxwell – while Firoz Kassam, Nick Merry, Tim Midgeley, and Robin Herd were interesting characters to have around too. Before United turned professional, the club president tended to cover many of the roles that the chairman of the board later took on, and United often had colourful incumbents of this position too. The club's first president after World War I was Major William Lauriston Melville Lee. In 1916 he was appointed head of PMS2, an organisation established by the Directorate of Military Intelligence Section 5 (MI5) to spy on the British socialist movement. Major Lee was responsible for 'setting up' members of the Socialist Labour Party, and was described by one of his agents, Herbert Booth, as 'a crank on Socialism'. The PMS2 was closed down in 1917 following a controversial court case, and Major Lee returned to his home in Stoke House, at the bottom end of Manor Road in Headington. Later that year he established and edited a journal called *Industrial Peace*, which circulated information on left-wing political organisations and individuals. Major Lee had the honour of performing the ceremonial first kick-off at the Manor in September 1925, and he remained as president until the summer of 1936. He died in 1955.

BUD MAY

HARRY Brian 'Bud' Houghton is almost certainly Oxford's only Indian-born player. He was born in Madras (renamed Chennai in 1996) on September 1st 1936 to a British father and an Indian mother, emigrating to Godalming aged 11, when India gained independence. He joined Bradford Park Avenue as an amateur when he was just 17, and in 1957 Birmingham City's manager Arthur Turner paid £5,250 for him. He rarely played for Birmingham and was off to Southend United a year later. In March 1961, Turner, now manager of Oxford, signed Houghton for £2,000 and was instantly rewarded with 13 goals in 14 games, including five against Boston. Houghton set several goalscoring records at United, including scoring in their first game in the Football League, before joining Lincoln City for £6,000 in October 1963. He went on to play for Southern League sides Chelmsford, Cambridge United, Wellington Town, and Cheltenham Town, before returning to Oxford where he played for Morris Motors in the Hellenic League. Houghton died in 1994.

A DISPOSITION FOR BENEVOLENCE

ON July 26th 2003, Oxford played Coventry City for the Bill Halsey Memorial Trophy; the game ended goalless with the Sky Blues eventually winning the penalty shoot-out 9-8. That was the last time that the trophy was played for, and allegedly it had to be retrieved from a groundsman's hut at Highfield Road from underneath a sack of line-marking powder. It was previously called the Oxfordshire Benevolent Cup and before that, until 1948, the Oxon Hospital Cup. United's first triumph in the competition came on May 13th 1939, when they beat Bicester Town 1-0 in the final. Headington also reached the final the following season, when they lost 4-3 to Pressed Steel. In 1948 United achieved what was possibly their best result at that time when they beat Oxford City 1-0 in the final, watched by 6,500, having earlier beaten Osberton Radiators 5-0 in the semi-final. City were avenged the next season, beating Headington 4-1 to lift the newly named trophy, while United beat City in the finals in 1961, 1962, and 1964. In October 1966 two professional clubs competed for the cup for the first time, when Leicester City visited the Manor and beat United 3-1. Crystal Palace provided the next three opponents, playing every two seasons with a draw, a win, and a defeat to show for it. The cup then reverted to local competition, with United playing Oxford City and Witney Town. After a gap of eight seasons, United again played against professional opposition, beating Cambridge United 2-1 in 1984, and this continued on an annual basis as a pre-season game until 2003. Highlights included a 4-0 win over AFC Bournemouth in 1987, a 2-0 defeat by QPR in the club's official centenary match in 1993, a Paul Moody hat-trick in a 3-2 win against West Ham United in 1995, a 3-1 win over Greek side Panionios in 1998 (the only time a non-English side has been involved), a 3-0 defeat by Birmingham City in 2000 (the game was nothing special, but it was interrupted for a few minutes by a female streaker who seemed intent on making friends with City keeper Ian Bennett), and a 1-1 draw with Crystal Palace (with United winning 5-4 on penalties) in the first ever game at the Kassam Stadium. This wasn't the first such cup in which United played; in 1925/26 the club entered the Chipping Norton Hospital Cup and reached the final, but lost 2-1 to Chippy, and the following season they were beaten 3-0 by Bicester in the final.

SUBS COMING UP

WHILE Paul Moody's hat-trick against Burnley on March 23rd 1996 remains a unique achievement for a United substitute, a number of substitutes have managed braces. The first to score twice off the bench was Neil Whatmore at Rotherham United in December 1983 in a 2-1 win, after coming on for Gary Barnett. This was followed by Chris Allen in August 1992, when he came on for Nick Cusack at home to Swansea City in a 3-0 League Cup win. This didn't happen again until December 2001, when Phil Gray scored twice in a 3-2 win over Mansfield Town after replacing Andy Scott, while on February 22nd 2003 it was Scott again who made way for Lee Steele who scored twice to win 3-2 at Torquay United after Oxford were 2-1 down. In April 2008, Matt Green came on for Craig McAllister to score a double in a 5-1 win over Farsley Celtic, while most recently Jack Midson scored twice on October 10th 2009, in a 5-0 win over Chester City after replacing James Constable, who had also scored two.

SENIOR MOMENTS

HEADINGTON'S first game in the Oxfordshire Senior Cup was in February 1901, when they lost 3-2 at home to Thame after a 1-1 draw. The following season the side reached the final for the first time, losing 3-2 to Culham College in a replay at the White House after a 0-0 draw. United didn't enter the competition again until 1922, when they again reached the final, losing 2-1 to Headington's great rivals, Cowley. The next few seasons saw United eliminated in the early rounds, frequently by their arch-nemesis Morris Motors, although they did reach the final again in 1930, when they were roundly beaten 8-3 by Oxford City's reserves. In 1936, United won the cup for the first time, beating Banbury Spencer 1-0 before a White House crowd of 5,000 in a replay following a 1-1 draw. After a couple of semi-final appearances, United's next final was in 1939, when Bicester Town won 2-1 with 5,906 in attendance. In 1942 Oxford City beat United 2-1 in the final, and City also beat Headington 4-0 in the 1946 final. United were avenged two years later, when they beat City 1-0 at Iffley Road before a crowd of 7,796. Since turning professional in 1949, United have mainly fielded their reserves in this competition.

LAST-MINUTE NERVES

ON May 2nd 1992, Oxford travelled to Tranmere Rovers needing at least a point, while hoping for an unlikely combination of results elsewhere, in order to avoid relegation to the Third Division. At half-time the game was goalless and other scorelines meant Oxford would be relegated if nothing changed. Second-half goals from Joey Beauchamp and John Durnin, coupled with an outstanding display from much-disparaged goalkeeper Paul Kee, earned United a 2-1 win, watched by a crowd of 9,173, including 2,000 supporting Oxford. Tranmere's goal was scored by former U's legend John Aldridge, his 40th of the season, which equalled Rovers' record. After the game it was still unclear if the win had guaranteed safety and, with the Oxford players on the pitch in front of the away end, there was an agonising wait while fans listened to their radios waiting for results from elsewhere to be announced. The news eventually came through that David Speedie had scored a hat-trick for Blackburn Rovers to beat Plymouth Argyle 3-1 and, amid much rejoicing from fans and players, United remained a Second Division side.

Before:

		P	W	D	L	F	A	Pts
18	Sunderland	43	14	8	21	57	61	50
19	Grimsby Town	44	13	11	20	46	60	50
20	Newcastle United	45	12	13	20	64	83	49
21	Plymouth Argyle	45	13	9	23	41	61	48
22	**Oxford United**	45	12	11	22	64	72	47
23	Port Vale	45	10	15	20	42	58	45
24	Brighton & Hove Albion	44	11	11	22	53	73	44

After:

		P	W	D	L	F	A	Pts
20	Newcastle United	46	13	13	20	66	84	52
21	**Oxford United**	46	13	11	22	66	73	50
22	Plymouth Argyle	46	13	9	24	42	64	48
23	Brighton & Hove Albion	46	12	11	23	56	77	47
24	Port Vale	46	10	15	21	42	59	45

DEMO CRAZY

OXFORD'S supporters occasionally feel the need to make their views known. They were particularly vehement in their opposition to Robert Maxwell's Thames Valley Royals scheme, when he tried unsuccessfully to get Reading to merge with United. The announcement was made on April 16th 1983, after Oxford had won 1-0 at Doncaster Rovers. The following Saturday, the club was at home to Wigan Athletic and before the game supporters, who had formed a group called SOS (Save Oxford Soccer) came onto the pitch and held a sit-down demonstration in front of the directors' box, many holding placards and banners opposing the scheme. It was a peaceful protest, and only threatened to turn ugly when Maxwell took his seat in the stand to a shower of invective, leading him to label the situation "a bloody disgrace". Nine days later Oxford were at home to Reading, with the kick-off switched to 11am on police advice. Nevertheless, U's supporters were up early to congregate at Oxford station ready to march to the Manor. Maxwell met the marchers at Gloucester Green bus station to try to explain to them his opinion that the merger was vital to stop the club from folding, but he was drowned out by cries of "Maxwell out". Another time that Oxford fans congregated to demonstrate their displeasure was on March 15th 2006. Club owner Firoz Kassam had just installed Bill Smith and Brendan Cross to take control of the day-to-day running of the club, leading to widespread speculation that a deal to sell the club to the Woodstock Partners Ltd consortium had fallen through. At the Wednesday evening game against Bristol Rovers, large numbers of Oxford supporters gathered outside the main entrance to the ground, while another group attended a meeting inside with Smith and Cross. Those outside the ground blocked the entrance to the car park when the coaches carrying Rovers supporters arrived, and then blockaded the road as the coaches moved to find an alternative entrance. However, when the Rovers fans expressed their support the Oxford fans were allowed onto the coaches to distribute leaflets and the coaches were allowed to proceed. Meanwhile, the meeting inside provided little cheer so a group of fans from outside stormed into the stadium and invaded the boardroom where visiting directors were sitting down to a pre-match meal. However, after distributing leaflets the protestors left and the rest of the evening passed off peacefully, with United winning 1-0 in Darren Patterson's first game as manager.

MANAGERIAL RECORDS AT OXFORD UNITED

Manager[1]	Highest Pos[2]	Promos	Releg[3]	Full Seas	Outcome
Harry Thompson	1st (SL)	0	0	9	Sacked
Arthur Turner	1st (D3)	3[4]	0	8	Made GM
Ron Saunders	20th (D2)	0	0	0	Moved
Gerry Summers	8th (D2)	0	1	5	Sacked
Mick Brown	11th (D3)	0	1	3	Moved
Bill Asprey	17th (D3)	0	0	1	Sacked
Ian Greaves	14th (D3)	0	0	0	Moved
Jim Smith	1st (D2)	2	1	3	Moved
Maurice Evans	18th (D1)	0	1	2	Resigned
Mark Lawrenson	N/A	0	1	0	Sacked
Brian Horton	10th (D2)	0	1	4	Moved
Denis Smith	17th (D2)	1	1	3	Moved/sacked
Malcolm Shotton	12th (D2)	0	1	1	Sacked
David Kemp	N/A	0	1	0	Sacked
Mark Wright	N/A	0	0	0	Sacked
Ian Atkins	8th (D4)	0	0	1	Sacked
Graham Rix	9th (D4)	0	0	0	Sacked
Ramon Díaz	N/A	0	0	0	Sacked
Brian Talbot	N/A	0	1	0	Sacked
Darren Patterson	9th (Conf)	0	0	0	Sacked
Chris Wilder	3rd (Conf)	1	0	1	Still there

Notes:

[1] Caretaker managers not included

[2] Division titles are old (pre-Premiership) style, and highest position refers only to final position in completed season; relegation seasons not included; N/A means manager wasn't in post for a full season

[3] Relegations are attributed to both managers for that season

[4] Includes election to Football League

COME ON YOU YELLOWS!

MATEO Andres Corbo Sottolano was one of Ramon Díaz's first signings, joining in January 2005. Corbo played 13 games for United, and while the left-sided defender didn't score, he did pick up an astonishing ten yellow cards. His first booking was on his debut against Yeovil Town, and he received his fifth yellow – and first suspension – in just his sixth game. He was shown his last two yellow cards (and therefore a red), picking up a further suspension, at Swansea on April 15th. Corbo's last appearance was against Chester City in the final game of the season, after which he walked out of the club after new manager Brian Talbot failed to call him in to a training session. He went to play in Australia for Newcastle Jets.

ON YOUR BIKE

JOHN Morris travels to Oxford's away games on his Vespa GTS 300 Automatic scooter, his itinerary including trips to Barrow and Gateshead. He also rode the 400-odd miles to Glasgow to watch United's pre-season friendly at Greenock Morton in July 2009 and Dumbarton in 2010. He is not the first person to travel to away games on two wheels; when United beat Wycombe 3-0 on April 8th 1996 half-a-dozen supporters rode to the game on their bicycles, including cycling up Hill Road, between Watlington and Christmas Common, with its average gradient of 1:18. A liquid lunch in Turville Heath was followed by one of United's most memorable away performances, making the following day's aches and pains well worth it.

FROM THE MANOR BORNE

UNITED'S last game at the Manor ground was a 1-1 draw against Port Vale on May 1st 2001, with Andy Scott scoring the U's last goal in front of an emotional crowd of 7,080. This was followed on May 13th by a valedictory game between the Oxford United Milk Cup-winning side and the QPR equivalents, with a few other old-boys also playing. The final match at the Manor was the John Byles Memorial Cup final between Garden City and Oxford City, on May 15th 2001. This was an under-16 tournament, in which the Kidlington side beat Oxford City 2-1. The ground was demolished later that year and the site is now occupied by the Manor Hospital.

OLD GUNS

GOALKEEPER Alan Judge is the oldest player to have played for United since the club turned professional, being 44 years and 176 days old when playing his final game, a 4-0 defeat at Southend United on November 6th 2004, making him the seventh-oldest player to have played in the Football League at the time. The oldest outfield player is Andy Linighan, who was 38 years 314 days when he came on as a substitute against Swansea City on April 28th 2001. Linighan is also the club's oldest debutant, being 38 years and 121 days when making his first appearance, at home to Luton Town. The side's oldest goalscorers are Gavin Johnson and Jimmy Bains, who coincidentally were both 36 years and 31 days old when they scored their final goals for the club; Bains' at Kidderminster in January 1956, and Johnson's at Wycombe in November 2006. They beat Guy Whittingham, who scored on his only appearance for United while on loan from Portsmouth in a 2-1 defeat at Swindon Town, at the age of 35 years 331 days.

GOING FOR GOALS

IN 1987/88 Luton did the double over Oxford with an aggregate score of 12-6, an incredible 18 goals; they beat United 5-2 at the Manor and 7-4 at Kenilworth Road, with Tommy Caton being substituted in the second game "to spare him further psychological damage". This equalled the record, as United and Corby Town shared 18 goals in 1958/59; Headington beat Corby 7-3 at the Manor on Boxing Day, and the following day United won 6-2 at Occupation Road. In 1954/55, United and Hastings Town managed 16 goals, Headington winning 8-2 at home, with the return game at Elphinstone Road going 5-1 to Hastings. In 2000/01, Oxford and Wrexham shared 15 goals as the Welshmen did the double over the U's; Wrexham won 4-3 at the Manor and 5-3 at the Racecourse. In 1957/58 United and Barry Town scored 14 goals as the U's won 7-2 at the Manor and 3-2 at Jenner Park. In 1961/62, Oxford and Gravesend also shared 14 goals; Alan Willey scored four as United won 8-0 at the Manor, while a Graham Atkinson hat-trick helped United to a 6-0 win at Stonebridge Road. Newcastle United and Oxford also managed 14 goals in 1991/92, with Newcastle winning 4-3 at home and Oxford winning the return match 5-2.

FIRST TIME LUCKY

WHEN Mark Creighton grabbed Oxford's winner against York City on August 8th 2009, he became the 59th United player to score on their debut, a trend started by Peter Roberts in the side's first professional game, a 5-2 defeat at Hastings on August 20th 1949 (United's other goalscorer, Ray Mansell, was on loan from Oxford City, but had played for Headington in the Spartan League the previous season). After joining the Football League, the side's first debutant scorer was Keith Havenhand, who was on target in a 2-0 win at York on December 21st 1963. Ron Johnston became the first debutant to score twice, getting both goals as United lost 4-2 at Bedford in the Southern League Cup qualifying round on August 19th 1950. This was bettered by Ken Smith, who hit a hat-trick on his debut at Bath City in the Southern League on August 22nd 1953. This feat was replicated by Joe Dickson against Boston on August 30th 1958, with Dickson going on to score eight goals in his first four games. On Boxing Day 1955, two debutants scored in the same game for the first time, as both Lionel Phillips and Billy Rees contributed to the 3-1 win over Kettering; Rees also scored in his next four games to record the best sequence for a new player. Peter Knight and Billy Simpson also scored in the same game on their debuts, a 3-0 win over Worcester City on August 20th 1960, but this deed wasn't repeated until Matt Green and substitute Ashley Barnes got the goals that beat Kidderminster 2-0 at Aggborough on November 24th 2007. The first substitute to score on his debut was David Rush, who scored a last-minute winner as Oxford beat Leyton Orient 3-2 on September 24th 1994. Another goalscoring sub was Mark Rawle, who scored with his first touch of the ball in Oxford's colours, 17 seconds after coming off the bench, to complete a 3-0 win over Swansea City on August 25th 2003 (all three goals were scored in the final five minutes). Another notable debut goalscorer was centre-forward Steve Anthrobus, who powered home a header as United won 2-1 at Stoke City on August 8th 1999. However, the Bus scored just three more goals in 69 appearances. Conversely, former Oxford City striker Guy Whittingham scored on his only appearance for Oxford, on loan from Portsmouth, as the U's lost 2-1 at Swindon on October 8th 2000.

DOING THE DOUBLE

UNITED won both the Southern League championship and the Southern League Cup in 1952/53, in just their fourth season as a professional outfit. This was, without doubt, the pinnacle of their achievements to date, although the season started slowly with just one win in their first four matches. United drew both legs of their Southern League Cup qualifying round against Hastings, enabling both clubs to qualify for the competition proper as the teams with the best results overall went through. The season really kicked off when Headington won 8-0 at Marlow in the FA Cup preliminary round; this was the first of five successive victories, including 4-2 over Aylesbury in the FA Cup and 2-1 against Bath City in the Southern League Cup. Two successive league defeats sandwiched further progress in both cups, before United beat Wycombe 6-2 in the FA Cup third qualifying round to earn revenge for their disqualification the previous season. Headington were eliminated from the FA Cup in the next round at Guildford, after which the U's went unbeaten in 16 successive league fixtures, including a 7-1 win at Gloucester that remains United's highest-scoring away win, and a 5-1 victory at Cheltenham. Meanwhile, United beat Guildford 3-1 in the Southern League Cup semi-final to set up a two-legged final against Weymouth. The unbeaten run was halted with a 1-0 defeat at Merthyr Tydfil, who scored when a freak bounce took the ball through goalkeeper Jack Ansell's hands. United stuttered slightly, with another defeat at Exeter City reserves following shortly afterwards, before they got the season back on track with a seven-game unbeaten league run. This included a 4-0 win over Chelmsford, which took Headington to the top of the league, and another 5-1 win against Cheltenham, this time at the Manor. In the first leg of the Southern League Cup final, 10,000 people saw United lose 2-1 at Weymouth after Arthur Turner had given Headington the lead. United were then beaten 4-2 at Bedford before the second leg. A record Manor crowd of 10,302 saw Bob Peart put United ahead and Norman Mills made it 2-0, but Weymouth equalised on aggregate in the last minute to take the tie into extra time, when Cyril Toulouse scored the winner in the second period. In their penultimate league game, United beat Gloucester 6-0, and in the last match of the season Headington beat Hastings 2-0 to win the title on goal average from Merthyr Tydfil, who had won the Southern League in the three previous seasons.

DIRTY LINEN

UNITED'S first season as a professional club, 1949/50, saw the side go 15 games before keeping their first clean sheet, a 2-0 home win over Bedford Town on November 5th. The following season the side went from September 9th to November 25th without keeping a clean sheet – another run of 15 matches. This was beaten in 1955/56, when Headington failed to prevent the opposition from scoring in 18 successive games, from December 10th until February 25th. In 1976/77 the run was increased to 19 games when United's defence was breached in every game from August 17th (the second match of the season, at Cambridge United in the League Cup) until November 23rd, when Oxford were beaten at home 1-0 by Southern League Kettering in the FA Cup first round replay, with Derek Dougan scoring the winner. This run was equalled in 1996/97, when United lost 2-1 at Oldham Athletic on November 23rd and didn't keep a clean sheet again until beating West Bromwich Albion 1-0 on March 8th.

TAPPING THE CLARETS

UNITED'S record against Chelmsford City is short, but notable. Their first meeting, on Boxing Day 1949, set a new crowd record for the Manor as 8,163 watched Headington win 2-1. As used to be the wont, the return game was played the following day, when Chelmsford secured their revenge with a 5-0 victory. The sides met five times during the calendar year 1957; in April, United did the double over the Clarets with a 1-0 away win followed three days later by a 2-0 home win, but the following September it was City that won both legs of their Southern League Cup qualifying round, 6-4 on aggregate. Chelmsford then compounded this ignominy by completing the double over United for the first time, winning 3-2 at the Manor later in September and 3-1 in Essex in February, thus becoming the only team to have beaten United four times in one season. When the sides met in the FA Cup first round in December 1967, they drew 3-3 at New Writtle Street and in the replay at the Manor they again drew 3-3 after extra time. The game went to a second replay, another first for United, played at Brentford's Griffin Park, and the Southern Leaguers won 1-0, Bill Cassidy scoring after just 45 seconds.

BIG RON MANAGER

ONE of United's best-known players, Ron Atkinson, also holds the record for the most senior appearances for the club, clocking up 561 games from his debut in a 3-2 win at Weymouth on August 22nd 1959, until his final match, a 1-1 draw at Fulham on October 12th 1971. Atkinson, who joined United from Aston Villa along with his brother Graham, was the first player to captain a club from non-league into the Second Division, leading Oxford to the Division Three title in 1968. He scored 21 goals in his time at the Manor before he left to become player-manager at Kettering. His strong performances in midfield earned him the nickname 'The Tank', bestowed by the Beech Road Stand denizens. After Kettering, Atkinson managed Cambridge United, West Bromwich Albion, Manchester United, Atletico Madrid, Aston Villa and Sheffield Wednesday, before he became a TV pundit. However, in 2004 he was forced to step down after uttering a racist word without realising that the microphone was still on. A man of many talents, Big Ron also released a single in 2002 in time for Christmas, entitled; It's Christmas... Let's Give Love A Try. Needless to say, it bombed. In 2007 he returned to Kettering as director of football, but the move lasted just four months before he returned to the media.

TAILS WE WIN

WHEN Oxford met Manchester United in the fourth round of the Milk Cup on November 30th 1983, people were surprised as the Third Division side drew 1-1 with the First Division giants thanks to Bobby McDonald's goal. The astonishment was widespread when Kevin Brock scored direct from a free kick as United drew the replay 1-1 at Old Trafford to earn a second replay. The Manchester chairman, Martin Edwards, offered to host the game, believing that Oxford would be grateful for the extra revenue, but United chairman Robert Maxwell was made of sterner stuff and insisted on the toss of a coin to decide the venue, even though the Manchester officials believed, erroneously, that both sides needed to agree to this arrangement. The toss was held via a conference call with the Football League the following day; Maxwell called tails, won the toss, and Manchester United had to return to the Manor for the second replay, which Oxford won 2-1 after extra time.

ON BEHALF OF THE COMMITTEE...

AFTER manager Harry Thompson was sacked in November 1958, following a 4-0 defeat at Hastings United in a Southern League Inter-Zone game, the Headington board decided not to appoint a caretaker manager while a replacement was sought, but instead opted to manage the side themselves. A three-man committee was established, featuring chairman Ron Coppock and board members Tom Lees and Tony Padley, who took charge of team selection and playing arrangements. The first game under this new modus operandi proved a triumph for the new-look management, as United beat Wisbech Town 5-1 at the Manor. The next game was an FA Cup second round tie at Peterborough United, then of the Midlands League, and widely considered the best team not in the Football League. Peterborough won 4-2 before a crowd of 16,855. The committee got back to winning ways in the next game, a 5-0 win over Rugby Town, followed by a 2-1 win over Hereford United. On Boxing Day, Headington beat Corby Town 7-3, winning the return match the following day 6-2; this was the final game before the appointment on New Year's Day of Arthur Turner. In total the record of the selection committee was: P6: W5 D0 L1 F27 A11

THE CAM OR DENIAL?

CAMBRIDGE City must have nightmares when recalling Geoff Denial. He scored a hat-trick as United beat City 3-2 at the Manor in the Southern League on February 6th 1960. This was Denial's second hat-trick against City that season, as he also scored all the goals as Headington won by the same scoreline at Milton Road in the FA Cup fourth qualifying round in October. United had also beaten City 3-2 in the away game at the City Ground in September, in which Denial had also found the net.

ODD-SHAPED BALLS

IT may come as a surprise to some, but United have played rugby. Twice, in fact. On October 11th 1958, Headington visited Oakfield, home of Rugby Town, and were mauled 4-1 in front of 1,100 spectators in a Southern League North West Section game. In the return at the Manor, United (who were then managed by a selection committee) won 5-0, with a slightly healthier attendance of 2,500.

SPARTAN DIET

BETWEEN leaving the Oxfordshire Senior League and joining the Southern League, Headington United spent two seasons in the Spartan League. Initially, United's application to join was rejected, so Headington instead opted to join the Reading & District Senior League. However, after being informed by telegram that a vacancy had arisen in the Spartan League, the club withdrew their application for the Reading League. Their first match at this higher level was a 2-1 defeat at Marlow on August 30th 1947, but this was followed by a 7-1 home win over Chelsea Mariners, a side based at a naval hostel in Chelsea. United's next game was an even more impressive 8-1 win at Hazells, from Aylesbury. Unfortunately, after this defeat Hazells resigned from the Spartan League and joined the more local Great Western Combination the following season; all their results, including a 7-0 defeat at Willesden and a 13-0 home defeat by Polytechnic, were expunged. On October 18th, United recorded their best result in the Spartan League, beating Leighton 12-0 at the Manor, with Jim Smith scoring four. A run of eight league matches unbeaten, culminating in a 3-0 win over eventual champions Willesden, took United to second in the table. However, despite winning their final game of the season 8-0 at Wycombe's Redford Sports, a defeat and two draws in their previous three games saw Headington slip away to finish fifth in Division One Western Section and miss out on promotion to the Premier Division. In their second Spartan season, Headington started disastrously, with an 8-2 defeat at eventual champions Slough Centre. However, this was soon forgotten as in the next match United beat local rivals Henley Town 6-0 at Reading Road. A couple of defeats were followed by a 5-0 win over Amersham and after a 2-0 defeat at Marlow, United went on a six-game winning run, including a 5-2 win over Luton Amateurs, completing the double over Henley with a 5-3 win at the Manor, a 7-0 drubbing of Chelsea Mariners, and a 6-0 win at Lyons Club, from Sudbury Hill, who finished bottom of the table. Later results were inconsistent, with a 6-0 win at Amersham and a 6-2 win over Lyons Club counteracted by second-placed Yiewsley completing the double, including a 5-1 defeat at Star Meadow. United's final game in the Spartan League was a 4-1 win over Chelsea Mariners, by which time Headington had decided to turn professional and had applied to join the Southern League.

HOT-SHOT SHELTS

GARY Shelton joined United from Sheffield Wednesday in the summer of 1987 for £155,000. During his time at United the Nottingham-born midfielder played 79 games over two seasons, scoring just three goals, bizarrely all against Leicester City (two in a 3-2 away win in the FA Cup, the other in a 1-1 home draw in the league). He left Oxford for Bristol City in a straight swap for future England manager Steve McClaren. The following season, 1990/91, Shelton played against Oxford twice. His goal tally against his former employers? Three! He scored City's goal when Oxford won 3-1 at home in November, and was on target twice in Bristol's 3-1 win at Ashton Gate in February. His scoring record with the Robins was much better than his record with United; he hit 24 goals in 150 league appearances. In 1992 Shelton had a brief spell as joint caretaker manager at Bristol City, and while he was on the coaching staff at Chester his son, Andy, was a player there.

WHAT'S IN A NAME?

ARTHUR Longbottom will possibly go down as having one of the silliest surnames of all United players. However, he is also the only one to have changed his name by deed poll. Longbottom signed for Oxford from Millwall in 1963, playing 42 games and scoring 16 goals for the U's, including four in United's 5-0 win over Darlington on October 26th 1963. He played 25 games in the same team as Alan Willey, but that's neither here nor there. He left Oxford for Colchester United in October 1964, ending his playing career at Scarborough the following year. After he retired he changed his last name to Langley. Another Oxford player who changed his name was Tanzanian full-back Eddie Odhiambo-Anaclet, who was born in Arusha but who moved to Oxford with his family as a child. More commonly known as Eddie Anaclet, he played for United's youth team, along with two of his brothers, Eric Odhiambo and Anaclet Odhiambo, but later joined Southampton before returning to the Kassam in 2006. In his two seasons at United, he scored six goals in 75 games. After leaving Oxford for Stevenage Borough in 2008, Eddie changed his surname to Odhiambo, to match his brothers, in tribute to his late father. In the east African Luo language, Odhiambo means 'born in the evening'.

HERD ABOVE THE NOISE

OXFORD chairman Robin Herd bought the club from Biomass Recycling in 1995, taking on the club's debt and the ongoing project to build a new stadium. Herd was an Oxford graduate, achieving the university's second-best exam result with a double-first in physics and engineering. He worked on the Concorde project for four years, becoming a senior scientific officer at just 24-years-old. He left to work for McLaren in 1965, moving to Cosworth three years later. In 1969 he co-founded March Engineering along with Max Mosley, Alan Rees, and Graham Coker (the name March was formed as an acronym of their surnames). He sold March in 1989 and quit racing altogether six years later when he bought United. At Oxford, Herd was able to achieve planning permission for the Minchery Farm site, but when the finances ran out with the ground a mere skeleton, Herd stood down as chairman and later sold his shareholding to Firoz Kassam, two and a half years after taking over. In 1999 he formed March Indy International as he attempted to get back into the racing industry.

CAMPEONES

ON May 16th 1984, the Manor hosted the 'battle of the champions', a game between Division Three winners Oxford United and Second Division title holders Chelsea. Chelsea had been out of the First Division for five seasons, while for United it was their first time back in the second tier since 1976. A crowd of 4,441 turned out to see goals from George Lawrence and John Aldridge earn the U's a 2-1 win. This wasn't the first time that United had been involved in a champions tussle. After winning the Southern League double in 1953, Headington played a Southern League Championship match against a team comprising the best players in the league. The Southern League composite side beat Headington 1-0 at the Manor after Headington had missed a first-half penalty and numerous chances to score in the second half. In August 1961 Oxford, having again won the Southern League, met Yeovil Town in the challenge match, Peter Knight and Ian McIntosh scoring for United in a 2-0 win. The following season Oxford had been elected to the Football League having again won the Southern League, and in the challenge match, United beat Cambridge United 2-0 with goals from Tony Jones and Bernard Evans.

BACK OF THE NET

OXFORD United's first presence on the information superhighway
was an unofficial site, now long defunct, called OxTales. It was founded
by Ian Turner in 1995 while he was at university in Norwich and was
reviewed in *Internet Today*, which called it; "quite possibly one of the best
footy fanzines I have seen in quite some time." Its url was www/aligrafix.
co.uk/oxtales.html. The first official site was launched on December 5th
1995, with the uninspiring address www.netlink.co.uk/users/oufc1/ and
it enabled United to become the first club in the Second Division to
have its own official website. The web address was changed to www.oufc.
co.uk in April 1998. The longest established independent website that
still exists is Rage Online (www.rageonline.co.uk) which was launched
in June 1999, initially to provide an online presence for the *Rage On*
fanzine, which has since ceased publication. Oxford's most popular, and
most populous, forum was This Is United, launched by the *Oxford Mail*
in April 2001 until its format changed and users left for the previously
dormant Yellows forum.

BARNEY'S DOOR

FORMER Headington United captain Vic Barney was one of the first
Englishmen to ply his trade in Serie A. Barney was an infantryman in
the British Army during World War II. After a battleground accident
he was sent to Naples for rest and recuperation and was soon put in
charge of looking after the Stadio Vomera. Barney, a 5ft 5ins. inside
forward, played at the stadium for some Army teams, and after the war
ended he was invited to play for Napoli at the newly renamed Stadio
della Liberazione. He spent one season at the Italian club and made
such a good impression that when he returned in 1992 for his golden
wedding celebrations, he was given a hero's welcome. Stepney-born
Barney moved to Oxfordshire and joined Headington in the summer of
1950, playing 93 games over his two seasons at the Manor, and scored
26 goals. A disagreement over the terms of his contract led to him being
given a free transfer to Guildford City in 1952, before he returned to
Oxford to work, play for, and coach Pressed Steel. He went on to coach
at Shipton-under-Wychwood and in his 70s – after having triple heart
bypass surgery – he still continued to coach at King's School in Witney.

TOP MEN

MANY of football's greats have played at Oxford, including some true legends. Nat Lofthouse played for Bolton in the FA Cup fourth round in 1953, the previous season's FA Cup finalists beating Southern League Headington 4-2 on a snow-covered pitch. On September 6th 1972, Oxford played host to Manchester United in the League Cup second round; the visitors featured players of the calibre of Bobby Charlton, George Best, and Denis Law, and required a 30-yard thunderbolt from Charlton to make the scores 2-2 and earn an Old Trafford replay, which the Red Devils won 3-1. In 2006, Manchester United played newly relegated Oxford in a pre-season friendly, with almost 11,500 turning up to witness Cristiano Ronaldo's first match since he competed in the World Cup finals with Portugal. Sir Stanley Matthews also trod the Manor turf. He turned out for an All-Star XI in a testimonial game for Jim Smith on October 17th 1956. Over 10,000 fans turned up to watch the All-Stars win 4-2, with 41-year-old Matthews showing, according to the *Oxford Mail*, "immaculate ball control, deceptive swerve, almost casual approach to a defender as if to say 'come and get it', sudden bursts of speed and slide-rule centres." Other greats to grace the Manor turf include Ian Rush for Liverpool, Paul Gascoigne for Newcastle United, and Gary Lineker for Everton, all in 1985/86.

PRISONER OF WHARTON

FRANK Wharton, who played for Headington United in the early 1930s, spent five years as a prisoner of war during the Second World War. On the commencement of hostilities, Wharton joined the Oxfordshire and Buckinghamshire Light Infantry. He was wounded in May 1940 in Boulogne, France, then captured and held in a German prisoner-of-war camp for five years. He was held in Stalag VIIIB in Lamsdorf and Teschen, Poland, before his release in 1945, when he returned to Oxford.

THREE FROM THE BENCH

THE only Oxford player to have come on as substitute and score a hat-trick is Paul Moody. He did this on March 23rd 1996 at home to Burnley, when he replaced David Rush with just 15 minutes remaining with United leading 1-0. Moody also made Joey Beauchamp's goal as the U's won 5-0.

JUST THE TICKET

OXFORD United play football; there has also been a play about Oxford United. On Thursday 12th and Friday 13th April 1979, the Temple Cowley School Drama Group put on a play at the Pegasus Theatre, Magdalen Road, entitled *Just the Ticket*, with the subtitle 'A Play for Oxford United'. The show was billed as 'A Football Fantasy?' and featured ten scenes, opening and closing at the Manor. The play was devised by the cast and director Mr D. Lovell, and concerned a group of schoolchildren's endeavours to attend a big match. Temple Cowley School closed down in 2003.

BOARD SILLY

TALISMANIC Northern Ireland striker Billy Hamilton was more than just a prolific goalscorer; he also turned his hand to designing board games. In 1985 Academy Games released his creation 'Billy Hamilton's Football Academy' to almost no fanfare whatsoever. The game is designed as a journey through the life of a professional footballer and is conducted in three stages: apprenticeship, professional, and gaining international caps. The apprenticeship takes three (game) years of learning the skills and demands of being a footballer, as well as performing the tasks essential to the everyday running of a football club. The Apprenticeship Stage is conducted by moving around the outer board based on the roll of a dice, performing actions dependent on which square the playing piece lands. After completing three circuits, the player trades Skill and Effort tokens for a potential rating that determines one of four paths to take through the Professional Stage. As a professional, the player becomes more involved in duties outside the game and must lend himself to charitable and promotional work. Progress through the Professional Stage is again dependent on the dice roll, with the square's actions detailed in look-up tables contained in the rule book. The idea is to proceed to the International Stage as quickly as possible, collecting goal tokens on the way. Once an international, the player could get the chance to lift the World Cup. In the International Stage players roll two dice (one giving advantages, the other penalties). Dice rolls can be changed by trading in goals gained during the professional phase. The winner is the first player to enter the World Cup Winner zone at the centre of the board.

CUP RUNNETH OVER

FOLLOWING United's 3-0 Milk Cup final victory over QPR, the players celebrated at the Bell in Beaconsfield, with their wives and the Milk Cup itself. As the players got off the coach back in Oxford the cup was in the possession of injured winger Peter Rhoades-Brown, who stuck it up his jumper and jumped in a taxi to stay with Kevin Brock in Abingdon, as somehow Brian McDermott took Rosie's jacket containing his house keys by mistake. The following day there was a panic at the club as no one knew where the trophy was. They phoned all of the players' houses, finally getting through to Brock's. When they awoke in the morning, Brock and Rhoades-Brown found themselves sharing a bed, with the Milk Cup between them. The cup was returned safely to the club and they embarked on an open-top bus tour of the city, ending at the Town Hall for a civic reception.

TORO! TORO! TORO!

THE ox head that features on United's badge was originally designed by Oxford director and anthropologist Desmond Morris in 1978, and used on shirts from 1979 to the present day, with a variety of wording and surrounding crests. In coming up with the design, Morris explained: "I replaced the old bull with a simple, powerful bull's head with a fiercely determined expression that was charging straight at you. The simplicity of the design meant that, not only could it easily be copied by fans, but it also showed up clearly at a distance, even when worn as a badge on the player's kit. Other clubs often have badges that are so complicated that you have to be very close to them to see the details and I wanted to avoid that." This replaced a round badge introduced in 1972, featuring a more realistic bull's head. The current crest surrounding Morris's Mycenaean-style ox was designed by a club employee and introduced in 2001 to coincide with a new kit design and the move to the new stadium. The first Oxford United badge had an ox crossing a ford inside a crest overlaying an 'H' for Headington. This was designed by Mr S. E. V. Clarke following a competition in the club's programme, for which over 60 entries were received. It was never actually used on the club's shirt.

HAMMERED

AFTER Oxford's final game at the Manor, many of the ground's fixtures and fittings were put up for auction, held at the ground on Saturday 9th June 2001. The auction, which had to be moved from the boardroom to the Beech Road terrace because so many people attended, raised over £10,000 for the club. Many people were there to buy their favourite seat from the Beech Road or Osler Road stands, while others bid up to £500 for some of the signage at the ground. The famous metal archway that stood at the entrance to the London Road passage was sold for just £100 to an Ardington resident. Malcolm and Brenda Warne from Somerset built a replica mini-stand in their back garden to house the seats they bought, while Jez Allen, who runs the Lancaster Bombers Bar in Cisnadioara, near Sibiu in Transylvania, carried over a number of seats to Romania on the back of his Land Rover.

BAGGIES TROUSERED

AFTER promotion to the top flight United's first game in the highest tier of English football was away to West Bromwich Albion on Saturday 17th August 1985. On their three previous visits to the Hawthorns, Oxford had lost every time and hadn't even scored. So there were extra celebrations among the 3,000 travelling fans when Bobby McDonald headed home the equaliser, to Imre Varadi's opener, to earn United's first point in the top flight. Eight years later Varadi would go on to play for Oxford, on loan from Leeds United.

MAD DOG'S AN ENGLISHMAN

MICKEY Lewis joined United from Derby County in 1988 as part of the controversial deal that took Trevor Hebberd from Kevin Maxwell's Oxford to dad Robert Maxwell's Rams. Lewis clocked up over 350 appearances for the U's in over 11 years, generally in midfield but occasionally in defence. After hanging up his boots, 'Mad Dog' became youth team coach and fulfilled a variety of roles, including on one occasion at Blackpool in August 1999, acting as physiotherapist. He became caretaker manager after Malcolm Shotton's departure and, more recently, assistant manager to Darren Patterson and Chris Wilder. In between he spent three years as coach to Oxford University, and was then David Penney's assistant at Doncaster Rovers.

FIVE TIMES LUCKY

IN the 1993/94 season Oxford and Tranmere Rovers met an astonishing five times in league and cup matches. The first meeting, at Prenton Park in the League Cup second round, first leg, saw Rovers thrash United 5-1 with Oxford's former hero John Aldridge netting twice and Pat Nevin grabbing a hat-trick. Four days later the sides met again on Merseyside for a Division Two game, with Tranmere winning 2-0. The second leg of the League Cup fixture was a 1-1 draw, ensuring that Oxford took no further part in that season's competition. The sides next played each other in the FA Cup third round at the Manor; this time the U's got some revenge for their League Cup mauling, progressing thanks to a 2-0 win. The fifth encounter of the season was the return league fixture at the Manor, which again Oxford won 1-0 to ensure that over the five matches honours were even, with two wins each and a draw. In 1959/60, United and Chelmsford City had met five times; in the Southern League Cup qualifying round both legs ended 1-1, which allowed both clubs to progress, and they met again in the second round, with the Clarets winning 1-0. The Southern League encounter at the Manor was a 0-0 draw, with Headington winning the return match 2-1. In 1982/83 Oxford and local rivals Reading met on five occasions, first in the Football League Trophy when Reading won 2-1 at Elm Park. The sides then met in the first round of the League Cup, United winning both legs 2-0. In the Third Division, Oxford won 3-0 at Elm Park, but Reading won the return game 2-1 in the midst of the Thames Valley Royals drama. Two seasons later Blackburn Rovers were United's recurring opponents. In the second round of the League Cup a 1-1 draw at Ewood Park was followed by a second-leg 3-1 win for Oxford, but Rovers were avenged when they beat the Yellows 1-0 at the Manor in the FA Cup fourth round. In Division Two, Oxford won 2-1 at the Manor and drew 1-1 at Ewood Park. In 2005/06, United and Cheltenham Town became regular opponents with four of the five meetings taking place in December. In the FA Cup second round the sides drew 1-1 at Whaddon Road before United won their League Two match 2-1 at the same venue three days later. Cheltenham won the FA Cup replay 2-1 at the Kassam before beating Oxford 2-1 in the LDV Vans Trophy third round in Cheltenham. The home league meeting was a 1-1 draw in February.

HERE'S HUGHIE!

HUGH McGrogan had the debut that most players can only dream about. The 17-year-old Dumbarton-born winger started at the Manor in a Second Division game against leaders Manchester United on February 8th 1975. United beat the title favourites 1-0 with a 25-yard screamer from Derek Clarke, captured by the *Match of the Day* cameras. McGrogan had joined United as an apprentice in 1972, and was part of the side that won the Midlands Youth League in 1974/75 before his promotion to the seniors in March 1975. In 1980 he joined Carlisle United, with Gary Watson, for £19,000, but he made just two appearances before returning to Oxfordshire to play for Witney Town. McGrogan died on Tuesday 1st September 1998 after the car he was driving smashed into Blackthorn Bridge on the A41 near Bicester.

AWAY THE LADS

TWICE in three seasons United made the long trip to Newcastle-upon-Tyne only to have the game called off because of the weather. The first time, on March 20th 1991, the game started but heavy rain forced a half-time abandonment with the score 1-0 to Newcastle, Mick Quinn the scorer in front of 9,858. The game was rearranged for April 10th, when Simpson scored twice in a 2-2 draw before a crowd of just 10,004. Two years later, on April 12th 1993, the team again made the journey to Tyneside, only for heavy rain to cause the game to be postponed about two hours before kick-off. The match was rearranged for Thursday 5th May and Newcastle won 2-1 after substitute Nick Cusack had given United the lead. The referee for this encounter was the aptly named Allan Flood.

NELLY'S IRRELEVANT

FORMER Oxford player Craig Nelthorpe played against United for three different clubs in the 2009/10 season. On the opening day he was a substitute as York City lost 2-1 at the Kassam Stadium; in November he started for Barrow in their 1-0 defeat in Oxford, and in February he came off the bench for Luton Town, who won 2-1 at Kenilworth Road. However, his spell at Barrow was classed as an 'emergency loan' so this was permitted under Fifa guidelines.

STERILE BEDDING

IN 1951/52 United's goalkeepers kept 20 clean sheets in the Southern League, plus one in the Southern League Cup and one in the FA Cup. Roger Ashton led the way with 12 shut-outs, future England keeper Colin McDonald had seven (including the two cups), and Tom Carpenter the other. This was bettered two seasons later, when Jack Ansell maintained 30 clean sheets in 58 appearances, 20 in the Southern League and 10 in the cups. Fellow keepers Les Clinkaberry and Ron Humpston both failed to prevent the opposition scoring. In the Football League, Harry Fearnley matched Ansell's league record of 20 clean sheets in 1964/65, but he failed to keep out his opponents in any of his four cup matches; Vic Rouse kept one clean sheet that season. United kept 21 clean sheets in 1969/70, with Jim Barron having 19 shut-outs (15 in the league) and Mick Kearns two. Roy Burton alone kept 21 clean sheets in 1981/82, of which 15 were in the Football League, while three seasons later Steve Hardwick kept 18 league clean sheets (plus one in the FA Cup). In United's Third Division championship season of 1995/96 the side kept 22 clean sheets, with Tim Carter keeping six (four in the league) and Phil Whitehead 17, of which 15 were league games. More recently, Billy Turley kept 20 clean sheets in the Conference in 2006/07, plus a further three in the FA Cup and FA Trophy. He followed this with a further 21 shut-outs, 19 in the Conference, the next season. Ryan Clarke kept 25 clean sheets in 2009/10, of which 23 were in the Conference. At the other end of the scale, in 2000/01 United managed to prevent the opposition from scoring in just six games, Richard Knight being the goalie in all six.

MR PERSONALITY

WHEN he was Oxford's manager, Malcolm Shotton was nominated by United supporters for the 1998 BBC Sports Personality of the Year award. Shotton, like the rest of the backroom staff, had worked for two months without pay in October and November 1998 as the club suffered a financial crisis. Despite receiving over 3,000 votes, Shotton didn't win the award; Michael Owen came first, followed by Denise Lewis and Iwan Thomas. However, the campaign to get him nominated earned the club a feature on *Football Focus* and a mention on *Match of the Day*.

THE TRAIN TOOK THE STRAIN

THE first recorded football special train for a Headington game was on April 1st 1899: for the replay of the Oxfordshire Shield final at Witney against Chipping Norton Swifts, after a 0-0 draw at Oxford City. A special train was laid on by GWR to transport nearly 500 Headington supporters from Oxford, the train being "full to inconvenience". Headington lost the replay 2-1, but the competition was later declared incomplete after the Swifts were found to have fielded two players, Webb and Juffs, who were Gloucestershire men, regularly playing for Moreton-in-Marsh in the Cotswold League. The Oxfordshire FA refused to award the Shield to Headington, but they did permit the club to mint its own medals.

PARKER'S PORRIDGE

TERRY Parker was the first Oxford player to have been sent to jail while on the club's books. Parker, whose contract was terminated for serious misconduct, was given an 18-month sentence for affray following a violent pub brawl in the Standing Order pub in Southampton on July 4th 2005. Parker, who pleaded not guilty, had a previous conviction in 2002 for a pub-related charge of battery. On June 4th 2010 Adam Chapman was sentenced to 30 months for causing death by dangerous driving.

MEDAL MAN

WHEN the club was suffering a financial crisis in 1998, Milk Cup winner Les Phillips donated his 1986 medal for auction. The medal was bought by the supporters group FOUL (Fighting for Oxford United's Life) for £1,100. FOUL returned the medal to Les on the Manor pitch at half-time of the FA Cup tie against Chelsea in January 1999.

MAGIC MUSHROOM

OXFORD forward Billy Hamilton was given the unusual nickname of Mushroom Billy. The giant Northern Ireland international striker used to pick the wild edible mushrooms that grew at Oxford's training ground. Other nicknames included Trevor Hebberd's 'Nijinksy' (because he had the stamina of the racehorse) and Gary Briggs' 'Rambo'.

DON'T TURNER BACK

HEADINGTON United appointed Arthur Turner as manager on New Year's Day 1959. On April 2nd 1959, Turner was offered the job of manager at First Division club Leeds United. At a specially convened meeting the following day, Mr Turner informed the Headington board that he was intending to accept Leeds' offer. One of the club's directors, Tony Padley, was appointed to act as a caretaker manager until Turner's successor could be recruited. On April 11th, another emergency meeting was held by the board, with members of the supporters club also present. This meeting decided that the Southern League club should outbid Leeds' offer, a move that so impressed Turner that he decided to remain with the club, which he then proceeded to manage from non-league to the Second Division in under ten years.

BACKROOM BOYS

SOME of the backroom staff at the Kassam Stadium have been with the club for many years. Youth and community officer Peter Rhoades-Brown joined United from Chelsea in January 1984, but injury forced him to retire almost five years later. He went to Australia for a year before returning to the club as community officer, a role he has performed ever since. He also played for Marlow for a spell, turning out against Oxford when the Isthmian Leaguers beat United 2-0 in the FA Cup first round in November 1994; an event for which Rosie received a standing ovation from the Oxford supporters at United's next home game. Les Taylor is Oxford's Youth Development Officer, having joined United as a youngster and coming up through the ranks. He was sold to Watford and captained their 1984 FA Cup final side. After spells with Reading and Colchester United he returned to Oxford in 1992 to become the under-16s coach. General manager Mick Brown has been with United since March 1982; he was appointed by director Peter Marsh in his last act before Robert Maxwell sacked him. Initially working as a youth liaison and commercial officer, Brown had been responsible for setting up the London Road Travel Club, which was initially run independently of the club. He became the ticket office manager when the office was built in what was formerly the pool room of the supporters' club, and Jim Hunt's assistant in 1987, becoming secretary in 1989. He assumed his current responsibilities in May 2007.

FAT MATT

MATT Taylor, who has forged an impressive career on the left wing and as wing-back at Luton Town, Portsmouth, and Bolton Wanderers, had an inauspicious start to his profession as a footballer. The son of an architect, he was born in Oxford and attended John Mason School, Abingdon. Taylor was in the side that won the 1995 under-13s Vale of White Horse Schools Cup and that reached the final of the Oxfordshire Schools Cup in the same year. As a boy he played for Quarry, based at the Quarry Recreation Ground where United, as Headington, had played their first games in 1893/94. Before joining Luton in 1998 he had a trial with Oxford United, but the U's rejected him on the grounds that he was too fat and recommended that he play in goal. Now he is a Premiership regular and has won three England under-21 caps.

DEGREES OF KELVIN

OXFORD United chairman Kelvin Thomas is no stranger to the coal face of the football business. Thomas's grandfather Bob played for Fulham and Crystal Palace, scoring 23 goals in Fulham's 1948/49 Second Division championship season, and Kelvin's cousin Geoff Pitcher spent three years at Watford after being a trainee at Millwall. Pitcher then spent three years at Kingstonian where he played alongside former United striker Dave Leworthy before joining Brighton & Hove Albion and then Havant & Waterlooville. Thomas was a player himself, mainly in central defence or central midfield. His first club was Dulwich Hamlet, but after only a few senior appearances he moved on to Croydon Athletic. It was at his next club, Banstead Athletic, where Thomas had most success, playing in the semi-final of the FA Vase in 1996/97, against Whitby Town. While a player, Thomas also worked for Charlton Athletic and then Crystal Palace as a Football in the Community coach. After leaving Banstead, Thomas moved to the United States, where he played briefly for South West Florida Manatees in Division One (the level below the MLS). He remained in Florida until his appointment as a business adviser with United, supporting Nick Merry and Jim Smith as a director of WPL in 2006. After returning to Florida for a while, he was invited back to Oxford as chairman in 2008, when he moved to Woodstock.

UNITY SCARF

WHEN the crisis group FOUL (Fighting for Oxford United's Life) started, it held a symbolic appeal to supporters of other Football League clubs to send a scarf to show their support for the continued survival of Oxford United. The idea was to join all the scarves together and stretch them as far round the Manor as possible. As well as receiving scarves from almost all the English league clubs, many others were sent in from supporters of non-league sides, as well as from Scotland and Europe. The scarf was featured on *Football Focus*, who referred to it as "the famous Oxford scarf of unity" and as well as making an appearance on the pitch at the Manor it was also sent to the *Fans United 3* event at a match between Chester City and Brighton, where it was shown on Sky Sports. The 400-metre-long scarf was paraded around the Deva pitch at half-time by about 200 volunteers and it stretched the whole way around the boundary of the playing area, the end bit still starting to snake its way round when the first volunteers had completed a lap of the pitch. As it was raining heavily that night the whole thing got soaked and it took two days to dry. After FOUL had considered the scarf had fulfilled its purpose, it was passed on to Wimbledon to be used as part of their anti-Milton Keynes franchise protest. They in turn passed it on to Bury and it was used as a general resource for fans' groups around the country until it eventually disappeared.

THE TRIANGLE

THE original drawings for the Kassam Stadium naturally depicted all four stands. When construction commenced the footings for the West Stand were put in place as they were for the other three stands, but the decision to proceed without completing the West Stand was taken early by United's managing director Keith Cox, on cost grounds. When construction recommenced after a four-year hiatus, during which time Firoz Kassam bought the club from Robin Herd, the other three stands were well under way, and Kassam decided that to commence the fourth stand, at a cost then estimated at £2.5 million, was not cost effective, and wouldn't be until crowds averaged 8,500 or more. So the Kassam remains three-sided with a 12,500 capacity.

IN THE KEY OF O

WHEN Oxford met Luton Town in the Blue Square Premier on September 8th 2009, the game was watched by a crowd of 10,613. Although this was not a Conference record attendance, it was considered respectable enough for Andy Anson, the CEO of England's 2018 World Cup Bid, to mention it in his keynote speech at the Leaders in Football conference at Stamford Bridge on October 8th 2009. Anson used the attendance to illustrate the passion in England for football, stating: "We all know that football is in our DNA. It is a passion that is deep-rooted and long-standing, and that will surface in every which way. Last month, there were World Cup qualifiers involving important European countries such as the Czech Republic and Denmark. The night before, there was also a Blue Square Premier League match between Oxford United and Luton Town. And I probably ought to explain that the Blue Square Premier League is non-league football. It is, in effect, our fifth division. So, which game do you think got the biggest crowd? Of course, Oxford against Luton, which was watched by more than 10,600 people. Yes, 10,600 for a non-league game… on a Tuesday night."

BOOTH'S THE TICKET

COLIN Booth held Oxford's Football League goalscoring record for 19 seasons after he scored 23 goals in United's Fourth Division promotion campaign in 1964/65. This record was eventually beaten by Steve Biggins, who scored 24 goals (including five in the League and FA Cups) as the U's won the Third Division title in 1983/84. Booth joined United from Doncaster Rovers for £7,500 in the 1964 close season, having previously played for First Division sides Wolves and Nottingham Forest. He featured in Wolves' championship-winning side in 1957/58 and won an England under-23 cap before his £20,000 transfer to Nottingham Forest in October 1959. On November 10th 1956, Booth equalled a record set by Aston Villa's Billy Walker in 1920 when he became just the second player to score four goals against Arsenal, in Wolves' 5-2 win at Molineux. This record was again matched in 1964 by Chelsea's Bobby Tambling, who became the only player to score four against Arsenal at Highbury. Booth's last game for Oxford was in November 1965 against Gillingham, after which he was forced to retire through injury. He then became a healthcare professional.

OUFC EUROPEAN XI

Lundin
(Sweden)

Sabin	Gnohere	Santos	Jeannin
(France)	(France)	(France)	(France)
Remy	Varadi	Karam	E'Beyer
(France)	(Hungary)	(France)	(Malta)
	Grebis	Sylla	
	(Latvia)	(France)	

LADS FROM KOSOVO COME AND GO

JUST before Firoz Kassam finalised his purchase of Oxford United from Robin Herd in March 1999, he asked a strange favour of club manager Malcolm Shotton. Kassam was a London hotelier who specialised in housing refugees and asylum seekers, and he asked Shotton if he could give a trial to six Kosovar refugees who were staying at one of his hotels in London. They were duly brought to Oxford for a morning of fitness tests followed by an afternoon of ball work. Unfortunately, none of the refugees were up to scratch; they were far too unfit to play professional football, and their ball work was equally below par. "We had a look at them, but decided none of them was quite good enough to play in the First Division," Shotton said.

CHESTER DRAWS

WHEN Chester City were expelled from the Conference on February 26th 2010 and had their results for the season expunged, it was the first time for the U's that one of their games was chalked off since a 0-0 draw with Chingford Town on October 21st 1950. United had beaten Chester City 4-0 at the Kassam Stadium on August 18th 2009, but the three points and four goals were struck from their record. In addition, James Constable scored a hat-trick in that game, but lost thosee goals. Apart from that match, United and Chester City had met 25 times, including one FA Cup meeting at the Deva Stadium when then non-league Chester beat League One United 3-2. The sides drew only two games, a goalless draw at the Manor in October 1978 and a 2-2 draw at Sealand Road in October 1981. Oxford were due to be Chester's next opponents the day after the Seals were voted out.

CELEBRITY FANS – GET THEM OUT OF HERE!

DEPENDING on one's definition of celebrity, Oxford are blessed with a number of supporters whose fame spreads beyond the Dreaming Spires. Possibly the most well known are children's TV presenter Timmy Mallet and sports broadcaster Jim Rosenthal. Manchester-born Mallet got hooked on the U's when he was a BBC Radio Oxford presenter in the early 1980s and he is still a regular at the Kassam. Rosenthal was famed for donning his ox-horn hat as he presented United's 3-0 win over QPR in the 1986 Milk Cup final, a moment that he described as "not the smartest career move", and the Oxford-born journalist, who started as a cub reporter with the *Oxford Mail*, was a member of the Gang of Four that tried to buy the club shortly after Firoz Kassam took over. The Oxford-based rock group Ride, consisting of Andy Bell, Mark Gardener, Laurence Colbert, and Steve Queralt, were fervent Oxford fans, turning up at five-a-side tournaments wearing specially made shirts in the red-and-black striped away colours featuring a badge of the ox head with RIDE embroidered where the Oxford United wording was supposed to go. They even inscribed the motto "Win or lose, up the U's" in the centre of their vinyl album Going Blank Again, which has appropriately just gone gold in UK sales. They used to stand with the Candyskins in 'popstars' corner' on the Beech Road shelf. Inspiral Carpets' lead singer Tom Hingley was born in Abingdon and was a U's supporter, while Britain's number one tennis player Tim Henman, from Weston on the Green, claims that he supports United. Eddie Jordan, owner of the Benson & Hedges Jordan Formula 1 team is another who numbers the U's among his sporting favourites, as does journalist and author Misha Glenny, who recalls being in Sarajevo listening to an Oxford game on the BBC World Service with bullets whistling around his ears. Radio presenter Dominik Diamond, although nominally a Celtic fan, adopted United after accompanying his friend 'Sad Andy' (Andrew Thompson) to the Manor. Richard Branson, boss of Virgin, is oft-rumoured to be an Oxford supporter, but it's his son Sam who is most often to be seen watching the Yellows. The late Professor Alan Raitt, one of the most distinguished British scholars of 19th-century French literature and whose work is referenced even by French experts – who died on September 2nd 2006 – was an Oxford season-ticket holder, as was the eminent economist Peter Donaldson, who died in September 2002, aged 67.

STRANGER DANGER

THERE are only four sides that have been in the Football League that United have not played since their election to it. Oxford replaced the defunct Accrington Stanley when joining the league in 1962, and it was the revived incarnation of Stanley that won promotion to League Two in 2006, as the U's were relegated to the Conference. Scarborough won promotion to the Football League just as Oxford reached the top flight, in 1985/86, but the Yorkshire side never rose above the basement division and were relegated on the last day of the 1998/99 season, when goalkeeper Jimmy Glass scored a last-minute goal for Carlisle United against Plymouth Argyle. Maidstone United played in the Fourth Division from their promotion from the Conference in 1989 until they went into liquidation in August 1992, while United were in Division Two. The only other Football League team that United haven't played is Milton Keynes Dons, formed in 2004 – nine months after Wimbledon moved to Milton Keynes – and starting life in League One, then a division above Oxford.

THE OX AND THE COW

WHILE most Oxford supporters maintain a healthy antipathy towards Swindon Town, the rivalry with the Robins is a relatively recent phenomenon. United's first real rivals were from a lot closer to home, as Headington and Cowley frequently crossed swords. Headington's first meeting with the Lilywhites was in the City Junior League in 1895, but it was after the First World War that the rivalry really intensified. In 1919/20 Cowley beat United 6-0 in the first round of the County Junior Shield, and they repeated the scoreline a month later, in Headington's first appearance in the Oxfordshire Charity Cup. The sides also met in the Oxford City FA Division One final, with 2,000 fans at the White House ground to see the Lilywhites win 1-0. Cowley produced an *in memoriam* card to celebrate the win and Headington's demise to a "severe bout of Cowleyitis". In 1922 the sides met in the final of the Oxfordshire Senior Cup, Cowley winning 2-1 with 3,200 present, and the following season Cowley beat Headington 8-0 and 6-0 in the Oxfordshire Senior League. In 1928 Cowley joined the Spartan League, becoming Oxford's second biggest club after City, but they returned to the county league in 1934. They disbanded in 1947, with Headington buying their main stand for £500.

NICK'S THE NAME

OXFORD United's current nickname of 'The Us' is often decried as lacking originality, but the club have been called that for over 50 years, so it at least has the benefit of longevity. The club's first nickname was 'The Orange and Blue' after the striped shirts that they wore. After Headington's first cup triumph – beating St. Mary Magdalene 1-0 after a 1-1 draw in the final of the Oxford City Junior Cup at the White House – the club's supporters marched back to Headington singing "Three cheers for the Orange and Blue". The village of Headington was up Headington Hill, a fairly steep climb from Oxford, and the football team came to be known as 'the boys from over the hill', although this was clearly too much of a mouthful to become a proper nickname. However, this geographical feature did lend its name to the club's next nickname, conferred by the local press in 1922, when they became known as "The Hillmen". This stuck for a few years before falling into disuse.

METRO MEN

HEADINGTON United were founder members of the Metropolitan & District League, formed in 1949 when United joined the Southern League and adopted professionalism. Because the local leagues refused to allow professional players to participate, United vice-chairman Professor George Keeton convened a meeting, along with Dagenham, to form a new reserve league. Initially called the Home Counties League until the Football Association refused to accept that name, its first chairman was Professor Keeton. In the first season the league was won by St. Neots & District, with Headington finishing fourth out of nine. The league expanded to 16 teams the following season, with United finishing seventh, but also winning the League Cup, beating Dagenham 1-0 in the final at the Manor. Headington were League Cup finalists again the following season, losing 6-2 to Tottenham at White Hart Lane. In 1953/54 United were the league champions and two seasons later they finished third and reached the League Cup final again, losing 4-1 on aggregate to Bedford. In 1962/63 Oxford United finished second, and the following season they finished fourth before they resigned to join the Football Combination. United had one further season in the Metropolitan League, in 1969/70, after the youth team failed to be re-elected into the South East Counties League.

HELLENIC HANDCART

AS well as the Metropolitan League, United were also founder members of the Hellenic League, formed in 1953. Headington fielded their 'A' team, comprising mainly 16 to 18 year olds, in this competition. In the inaugural season, Headington finished sixth out of 16 and reached the League Cup semi-final. The following season they had a mid-table league finish, but won the League Cup, beating Witney Town in the final. In 1955/56 the league was expanded to 18 teams, and Headington responded by becoming champions. The youth team continued to perform in the Hellenic League, from 1961 combining it with the newly formed Wessex League which comprised mostly Football League clubs, and which appealed to United because the games were played in midweek. Following a couple of mediocre seasons in the Hellenic League, United decided to resign at the end of the 1966/67 season and join the South-East Counties League instead.

PAYING THE PENALTY

JIM Magilton was one of Oxford's most reliable penalty takers. Of his 42 goals for United, 17 were from the penalty spot (and a good number more came from his deadly direct free kicks). He missed just once, in a 2-0 win over Derby County on November 13th 1993, but he made amends by scoring direct from a free kick later in the game. Magilton scored from open play in his last game for United, a lob over Leeds United goalkeeper Mark Beeney, to earn Oxford an extra-time FA Cup win. In the next round against Chelsea, Oxford were awarded a penalty when 2-1 down with five minutes remaining; with Magilton having left for Southampton for £600,000 the previous Friday, captain Mike Ford took the spot kick and blasted the ball against the bar. Another deadly penalty-kick taker was defender Andy Crosby. Of the 13 goals he scored for the U's, 11 were penalties, and he never missed one, typically putting the ball high into the net beyond the keeper's reach. This section wouldn't be complete without mentioning Rob Duffy's record. His first goal for United was a penalty on his debut against Halifax Town in August 2006, and of his 21 goals that season nine were from the spot (plus another in the penalty shoot-out against Exeter City in the play-offs), with four of his six goals the following season being penalties. He missed just once, at Southport in March 2007.

BLOWING IN THE WIND

UNITED'S record signing is Dean Windass, who joined Oxford from Aberdeen for £470,000 on July 10th 1998. Windass, who once famously received three red cards in one game while at the Dons, was signed by Malcolm Shotton, who knew him from their time together at Hull City. Windass scored on his United debut at Bristol City on August 8th and scored 18 goals in his 38 games for the U's. His final game for the Yellows was at Loftus Road on March 3rd 1999, but by that time it was already clear that he was about to leave and his performance was obviously affected by that. He left for Bradford City for £950,000, with a further £50,000 received at the end of the season after the Bantams were promoted to the Premiership. His sale enabled Oxford to pay Aberdeen the money for his transfer, which the Scottish club had kindly allowed Oxford to pay in arrears. United had previously rejected a £700,000 offer for Windass from Huddersfield Town. Windass was released by Hull City manager Brian Horton at the age of 18 but they gave him another chance four years later, after Horton had moved on to manage Oxford. It was from Hull that Windass moved for £700,000 to Aberdeen, where he received seven red cards in under three seasons, including those three in a match against Dundee United; he was red-carded for a bad tackle, then received another red card for swearing at the decision to dismiss him, and a third red for throwing down the corner flag as he marched off down the tunnel. He was given a six-match ban for his tantrum.

SELLIOTT

THE most that Oxford have received for a player is the £1,600,000 that Leicester City paid for central defender Matt Elliott on January 18th 1997. Elliott made 181 appearances for United after joining from Scunthorpe United for £150,000 on November 5th 1993. He scored 25 goals for United, an excellent record for a defender, including a 40-yarder at Carlisle United in February 1996 and a volley against Swindon Town a month later. Many Oxford fans claim that it was Elliott's sale that began the club's subsequent decline. After joining Leicester, Elliott captained them in the Premiership, and as a result of his father's background, the Roehampton-born stopper won 18 caps for Scotland.

DEAN WINDASS — UNITED'S RECORD SIGNING

MAXWELL'S HOUSE

OF all the characters to have been involved with Oxford United, the larger-than-life figure of Robert Maxwell is probably the most enigmatic. He was born with the name Ján Ludvík Hoch to Jewish parents on June 10th 1923 in Slatinské Doly, then in Czechoslovakia, now in Ukraine. He fled the Nazis and arrived in England in 1940, aged 17. He was awarded the Military Cross in 1945 for his work with British Intelligence (who gave him the name Ian Robert Maxwell), and after the war he went into business, buying small publishers Pergamon Press and building them into a major publishing house. He was elected as Labour MP for Buckingham in the 1964 general election, but lost his seat in 1970. By this time he was already resident in Headington, attending occasional Oxford United games and even offering to loan the club money (an offer that the club declined). In 1981, Maxwell acquired the British Printing and Communication Corporation (BPCC) and in 1984 he bought Mirror Group Newspapers. In December 1981 he was alerted to the plight of United by one of his employees, whose son Bob Oakes worked for the club, and although on holiday in the West Indies, Maxwell managed to forestall Barclays Bank, who were threatening to have the club wound up if they weren't repaid their overdraft of £150,000 (which United had already exceeded by £31,000). After returning from his holiday Maxwell studied the club's books and injected £121,000 into it, becoming chairman on January 6th 1982. Maxwell was hailed as a hero by the club's relieved supporters, but just 16 months later he was the villain after mooting the doomed Thames Valley Royals scheme (see elsewhere). Many considered that this was a move to blackmail the local council into agreeing a site for a much-needed new stadium, but it failed, as did Maxwell with his promise that he would step down if the merger didn't proceed. Maxwell then oversaw the two most successful seasons in the club's history as United became the first side to win the Third and Second Division titles in successive seasons and found themselves in the top flight for the first time. In the meantime, Maxwell had a £10 million bid for Manchester United rejected, but he did buy Derby's Baseball Ground and clear their debts, while installing his son Ian and daughter Ghislaine on the Oxford board. Ian later left to become chairman of Derby, to be replaced by his brother Kevin.

ON May 31st 1987, Robert Maxwell resigned the chairmanship of Oxford to take over at Derby, with Kevin becoming United's chairman, at least nominally. Maxwell died on November 5th 1991, when he fell overboard his yacht, *The Lady Ghislaine*, in the Canary Islands. His body was found by a local fisherman shortly afterwards and Maxwell was buried at the Mount of Olives in Jerusalem, Israel. Meanwhile, his son Kevin remained in charge at Oxford while his father's empire collapsed around him. He announced in December 1991 that the Maxwell family would be unable to keep the club running, with United losing an estimated £12,000 a week, and on December 5th Ghislaine resigned from the board. In May 1992 the club was sold to Jardine Mathieson, and registered in the name of Energy Holdings Ltd. Kevin was declared bankrupt with debts of £406.5 million in September 1992, becoming Britain's biggest personal bankrupt, but he and Ian were cleared of defrauding pensioners when the *Daily Mirror*'s pension fund went bust.

FOOTBALL CRAZY

WHEN Oxford played Bury on February 21st 2004, among the spectators was possibly the most glamorous woman to have attended a United game. Joan Collins, film star, author, and leading lady of *Dynasty*, had earlier that day conducted the ceremonial opening of the nearby Ozone cinema and, as a guest of chairman Firoz Kassam, she attended that afternoon's game. Whether she knew the rules or understood the significance of Dean Whitehead's equaliser in the 1-1 draw isn't known.

BAD BUY?

LEE Bradbury was subject to the single most expensive transfer fee of any Oxford player when Manchester City bought him from Portsmouth for £3 million in 1997. He was sold by City to Crystal Palace for a further £1,500,000 and in total his transfer fees added up to £4,800,000. Bradbury joined United from Walsall on a free transfer in June 2004, but his departure from Oxford, in January 2006, was subject to controversy. Bradbury had played 29 games in 2005/06 and one more appearance would have triggered a clause in his contract offering him an automatic one-year extension. However, manager Brian Talbot refused to play Bradbury again, and he eventually left for Southend United while Oxford tumbled out of the Football League.

DEANO'S TRAVELS

WHILE Lee Bradbury was subject to the single largest transfer deal of any United player, the player with the highest combined transfer fees is Dean Saunders. In a career spanning 20 seasons, Welsh international striker Saunders' transfer fees totalled a whopping £10,610,000 during his football career, which took in a number of top English and European clubs. The first money paid for him was when Oxford bought him from Brighton & Hove Albion for a modest £60,000 in March 1987, after he had joined the Seagulls from Swansea City on a free transfer. That fee proved to have been a bargain, as in October 1988, after 73 appearances and 33 goals, Kevin Maxwell's United sold him to dad Robert Maxwell's Derby County for £1 million in a move that led directly to Mark Lawrenson's departure as Oxford's manager. He moved from Derby to Liverpool three years later for £2.9 million, then a year later to Aston Villa for £2.3 million. After three years at Villa he joined Turkish side Galatasaray for £2.35 million, but one year later was back in Blighty, joining Nottingham Forest for £1.5 million. He moved to Sheffield United on a free transfer one year later, and after one year at Bramall Lane he was off to Benfica for £500,000. His final move was a free transfer to Bradford City.

AND CLOSE AS THIS

WHEN Oxford won the Third Division in 1968, it was achieved on the last day of the season. David Sloan scored the only goal as United beat Southport 1-0 on May 11th in front of a Manor crowd of 14,038. This gave the U's a one-point lead over Bury, who beat Watford 2-0, and a two-point lead over Shrewsbury Town, who won 2-0 at Gillingham. United's total of 57 points remains the lowest for a Third Division title winner.

	P	W	D	L	F	A	Pts	GAv
1 **Oxford United**	46	22	13	11	69	47	57	1.47
2 Bury	46	24	8	14	91	66	56	1.38
3 Shrewsbury Town	46	20	15	11	61	49	55	1.24
4 Torquay United	46	21	11	14	60	56	53	1.07
5 Reading	46	21	9	16	70	60	51	1.17

MOONLIT NIGHTS

EVEN before United turned professional and joined the Southern League they were known to take their training very seriously. At the start of 1948 the club was given permission to use the school in Margaret Road, Headington for physical training on Monday nights, and appointed a qualified instructor to lead the sessions. In addition, despite being amateurs, several nights a week the first eleven, reserves, and minor league players would turn up at the Manor, get changed, and go for a run of several miles around Headington. On their return to the ground they would have a hot bath and finish up with a fish and chip supper. They would frequently go out onto the Manor pitch to carry out ball practice by the light of the moon, until floodlights were installed in December 1950.

HARPER'S BIZARRE

TONY Harper was probably the first Headington player to join the Football League. He was spotted by Brentford's Andy Wilson while playing for United against Chelsea Mariners in London on March 6th 1948; a game that United won 4-1, and in which Harper scored. As well as Headington, whom he joined aged 14½, Harper played for MPRD and Oxford City, but at the end of the 1947/48 season the robust half-back signed amateur forms with Brentford. He was at Griffin Park until he rejoined Headington in the summer of 1955, and was a regular in their Second Division side of the early 1950s, until suffering relegation with them to the Third Division (South) in 1954. Back at the Manor he went on to play 138 games, scoring six goals over the next four years, before hanging up his boots in September 1959. Harper died in 1982.

THE PRICE IS WRONG

GEORGE Price played for Headington United for the 1926/27 season. He played for a number of local clubs, including Oxford City and Cowley Lilywhites, as well as Headington. He claimed that he never played without three or four pints inside him, but this obviously had a negative effect on his performance, such that he was told that if he ever went onto the pitch drunk again he would be kicked out of Headington. Perhaps that's why he lasted just one season.

NOT FOOD FOR THOUGHT

FOOTBALL catering is not often a gourmet experience, but the food on offer at the Manor was worse than most. In a 1998 survey of food at the 92 Football League grounds, sponsored by Colman's and edited by Jim White, Oxford's fare came in 88th place, just four above bottom-placed Leyton Orient. The excuse offered by the club's catering company Market Place Catering that it was "unfair to compare Oxford with a club like Manchester United" fell rather flat considering that little Cambridge United, with an average attendance less than half of Oxford's, came top of the survey. The report was particularly scathing about the standard of the hot dogs, calling them: "close to a local scandal: so small it gets lost in the hand, luke-warm, in poor bread, the sausage itself watery, floury, anything but meaty of taste..." The only surprise is that there were four clubs who offered fare even worse.

GROB'S UP!

WHEN Oxford's regular goalkeeper Phil Whitehead was injured in September 1997, manager Denis Smith moved quickly to sign a replacement. Unfortunately, the player he chose was 39-year-old Zimbabwean international Bruce Grobbelaar, who had just been charged by the Football Association for breaking its rules on betting, having one month previously been cleared of match-fixing charges at Winchester Crown Court and having similar charges dropped by the FA. The 39-year-old keeper signed on non-contract terms and was ready to play against Sheffield United the following weekend. However, youngster Elliot Jackson took part in the 4-2 home defeat instead, as Sheffield Wednesday nipped in to pay United £5,000 for Grobbelaar, six days after he signed.

NOT TAKING LE TISS

IN October 1983 United gave a trial to 16-year-old Matthew Le Tissier from Guernsey. He was invited because of the good impression his brother Kevin made in the reserves a couple of seasons earlier. In the same group was Simon Stapleton, who later played for Wycombe Wanderers. Unfortunately, Le Tissier failed to impress and he was released. On his way home he had a trial with Southampton. He stayed there for 16 years, won numerous accolades, and was awarded eight England caps.

FIRST DOWN

OXFORD suffered their first-ever relegation in 1976. A disastrous start to the season saw them win just one of their first nine league games, which included a sequence of six consecutive defeats. From mid-December until the end of February, United went 11 games without a win, picking up just six points. Although things picked up slightly with a run of four successive wins in March, the U's lost their last three games to finish third from bottom, four points behind Carlisle United. This ended eight seasons in Division Two and led to eight years in Division Three, with little indication during the late 1970s of the glory years that were to follow.

15. Blackburn Rovers	42	12	14	16	45	50	38
16. Plymouth Argyle	42	13	12	17	49	54	38
17. Oldham Athletic	42	13	12	17	57	68	38
18. Bristol Rovers	42	11	16	15	38	50	38
19. Carlisle United	42	12	13	17	45	59	37
20. Oxford United	**42**	**11**	**11**	**20**	**39**	**59**	**33**
21. York City	42	10	8	24	39	71	28
22. Portsmouth	42	9	7	26	32	61	25

GROUNDS FOR A MOVE

THE move to the Kassam Stadium in 2001 was the ninth time that United had changed grounds. When Headington was formed in 1893, they played their first home games on Quarry Recreation Ground, between Margaret Road and Ramsay Road. The following year – their first season in competitive football – they moved to Wootten's Field, now covered by Stephen Road, where they remained for four years. In 1898 Headington FC moved to Sandy Lane, on virtually the same site as the Manor, but four years later they moved to the other side of London Road, to the Britannia Field, now occupied by the northern end of Lime Walk. They played there for seven years, playing some home games at Highfield, returning to Sandy Lane for one season in 1909. They then returned to Quarry Rec, where they remained until World War I. After the war, United played back at Sandy Lane, moving up the road to the Paddock in 1922. In 1925 they moved to the Manor, where they remained for 76 years.

ODE DEAR

DESPITE the best efforts of some versifiers, there is a dearth of good football-related poetry. This was something that the Oxford United website Rage Online attempted to rectify with its 'Crap Poetry' page. Based on the concept that it is virtually impossible to write decent poetry about football, the site gathered the largest collection of United-related verse, producing over 30 examples of the orthometric muse. These included *Ode to an Angel*:

> "The small but gifted winger
> recalls, as he rounds his fourth defender
> and leaves him prostrate behind,
> with the empty goal at his mercy,
> that he is allergic to the potent mix
> of sweat and Old Spice
> and, having shaved that morning,
> he fluffs his shot entirely."

And William Wordsworth:

> "I wandered lonely as a cloud
> Who follows Oxenford from vales and hills,
> When all at once I saw a crowd
> Of ghosts in yellow and black frills;
> Upon the Manor is where you seek 'em,
> Fluttering and dancing round Joey Beauchamp."

PENNY FORUM

THE first fans' forum at the club was held by Kevin Maxwell in December 1990. They have been held ever since, with varying regularity and various levels of animation. Memorable moments include Keith Cox's tirade at *Rage On* fanzine editor Paul Beevers, which was even reported in the Guardian; Joe Kinnear's alcohol-fuelled expletive-laden rant; Firoz Kassam receiving a standing ovation for his promise that he wouldn't sell the club and stadium separately, just weeks before he did exactly that; and Simon Lenagan's struggles to come to terms with Powerpoint.

KNOCK BACKS

ALL players suffer from injuries, not always during a game. Mike Ford missed the first five months of his Oxford career with a back injury, somehow sustained on his honeymoon in the summer of 1988. Another victim was diminutive striker Ben Abbey. He joined Oxford from Crawley Town for £35,000 on September 29th 1999, but on his first day as a professional footballer he had to visit casualty after hitting himself between the eyes with a cricket bat. "I was playing with some of the youth lads and was batting," Abbey explained. "Somehow, I managed to hit the ball and on the follow-through caught myself right between my eyes. I had a big bruise and in training I couldn't really see anything and kept giving the ball away because I couldn't react quickly enough. It was the first time I had ever played cricket." Striker Billy Hamilton's career was ended by an injury he picked up in a pre-match warm-up against Blackburn Rovers in the FA Cup fourth round on January 30th 1985. Hamilton stubbed his toe and had to be replaced by Mark Jones, and he didn't play again until March 9th. He saw out the end of that promotion season and the start of United's First Division campaign, scoring twice in the 5-0 win over Leicester City, but after playing in the 1-0 home defeat by Sheffield Wednesday on August 31st, Hamilton suffered a relapse and didn't feature again until April 1986. He scored one of the goals in the 3-0 win over Arsenal in the final game of the season that earned the U's another year in the top flight, but featured just twice the next season before hanging up his boots. Of the 20 goals that Hamilton scored, just three came after his toe injury.

FRIENDS? OR MARRIAGE?

OXFORD had arranged to play QPR in a pre-season friendly on July 19th 2008; however the game had to be cancelled after it was discovered that the stadium had been double booked, and a wedding reception had been organised by the management company at the Kassam Stadium on the same date. Rather than upset the happy couple, the friendly did eventually go ahead against QPR on July 24th 2009, with Rangers managed by United old-boy Jim Magilton. The game ended 2-2, with United twice coming back from behind with goals from a Matt Green penalty and Jack Midson.

SCORES ON THE DOORS

THE current electronic scoreboard at the Kassam Stadium is nothing to shout about, with its two lines of 12 characters each, compared with scoreboards *passim* at the Manor. The first that was erected, in 1974, included an analogue clock in the top corner, and revolving numbers for the team scores. This occasionally led to the sight of the numbers going all the way round to get back to the beginning, causing some rather interesting scorelines to be displayed. The scoreboard, with the motif 'Never a quarrel – bet with Coral' prominently displayed, was badly damaged (along with the roof of the Osler Road stand) in the high winds of January 3rd 1976, and then in August 1980 the constant winding of the numbers led to the motor burning out. It was repaired free of charge by a United supporter and continued to function until it was decommissioned in the summer of 1985, when the whole of the Osler Road side was redeveloped on promotion to the First Division. It was replaced in March 1986 by a digital clock, initially positioned on the front of the police control box at the rear of the Cuckoo Lane End before being moved to the roof of the Osler Road terrace. The clock alternated between telling the time and the temperature, often causing great annoyance for those checking how long of a game remained only to discover that it was eight degrees Celsius. On September 23rd 1992, Oxford became the first club in the country to install a videowall, consisting of several large video screens affixed to the front of the Cuckoo Lane police control box, with a couple of smaller screens attached to the inside of the roof in the London Road stand. The videowall was upgraded in April, when the screens were made larger and the gaps between them made smaller, and eventually the whole concept was sold to Wolves.

SLOPING AWAY

THE pitch at the Manor was famous for its slope, which dropped eight feet from the corner of Osler Road/Cuckoo Lane to the corner of Beech Road/London Road. Many people claimed that the slope gave United a big advantage, and whenever they won the toss they chose to attack the Cuckoo Lane end in the first half, therefore going down towards the London Road after half-time.

COPPER AWARDS GOAL

WHEN Oxford visited Walsall on March 14th 1981, the U's won 3-0 after being 1-0 ahead with three minutes remaining. United's second goal was controversial; the ball appeared to strike the arm of Keith Cassells and many players stopped for a free kick. The Walsall goalie, Ron Green, rolled the ball out to take the kick, but Cassells nipped in and kicked the ball into the empty goal. The referee, R. Banks, allowed the goal after conferring with a police inspector. Apparently several players claimed that they had heard the whistle for the handball, but the referee denied blowing his whistle so he asked the inspector if he had heard anything. The policemen replied that he had not heard any whistle from the crowd and so the goal stood. Mark Jones had opened the scoring with his first goal for the U's, and Peter Foley scored the third.

PERFECT PITCH

THE pitch at the Kassam Stadium has been inspected by officials of both Real Madrid and Juventus. Both teams wanted to look at the underlying structure of the turf, which had been specially treated to be able to cope with the rigours of rugby and football. The pitch was a totally new design, with a mesh of drainage pipes covered first with a membrane and then with a combination of a biodegradable plastic grid and natural grass. The party from Madrid, which included Spanish goalscoring legend Emilio Butragueño, visited in February 2002 and was looking at using a similar system at the Bernabeu, while the Juve group, which arrived in July 2002, included Virginia Costa, the turf manager for Italy's Serie A.

BLUE HERON

BRIAN Heron must be one of the unluckiest players to have pulled on Oxford's yellow shirt. The popular Scottish winger joined United from Dumbarton for £20,000 in summer 1974, but in October 1975 he broke his leg in a 1-0 win at Notts County. On April 14th, Heron made his comeback in a reserve game against Fulham, but within five minutes of the start he broke his leg again and didn't play in the first team until March 1st 1977. After recovering, he played just four more games for Oxford before leaving for Scunthorpe United.

BLOWING IT

UNITED have blown promotion from good positions frequently in recent seasons. In 1994/95 Oxford were top after winning 4-1 at Peterborough United on Boxing Day, only to fade away and finish seventh in Division Two, outside the play-offs.

26/12/94		P	W	D	L	F	A	Pts	GS
1	**Oxford United**	21	14	4	3	41	22	46	41
2	Birmingham City	21	12	7	2	38	13	43	38
3	Wycombe Wanderers	21	12	5	4	32	24	41	32

06/06/95		P	W	D	L	F	A	Pts	GS
5	Huddersfield Town	46	22	15	9	79	49	81	79
6	Wycombe Wanderers	46	21	15	10	60	46	78	60
7	**Oxford United**	46	21	12	13	65	52	75	65

ON December 28th 2003, United's 1-0 win at Southend United took them two points clear at the top of Division Three, but again Oxford fell away, not helped by Ian Atkins' departure, and again they missed out on the play-offs.

28/12/03		P	W	D	L	F	A	Pts	GD
1	**Oxford United**	24	14	9	1	38	16	51	... 22
2	Doncaster Rovers	24	15	4	5	44	21	49	... 23
3	Hull City	25	13	8	4	48	24	47	... 24

08/05/04		P	W	D	L	F	A	Pts	GD
5	Mansfield Town	46	22	9	15	76	62	75	14
6	Northampton Town	46	22	9	15	58	51	75	7
7	Lincoln City	46	19	17	10	68	47	74	21
8	Yeovil Town	46	23	5	18	70	57	74	13
9	**Oxford United**	46	18	17	11	55	44	71	11

IN 2006/07 United were top of the Conference after their 0-0 Boxing Day draw with Woking, but their fall had already started and they finished second, 14 points adrift of Dagenham & Redbridge, before losing to Exeter City in the play-off semi-finals.

STAYING UP

ON the other side of the coin, United have survived relegation by the skin of their teeth on a few occasions. In 1973/74 the side earned the point they needed to survive the drop with a 0-0 draw at Millwall on the final day of the season, although Alf Woods missed an open goal for the Lions in the final few minutes.

		P	W	D	L	F	A	Pts	GAve
18	**Oxford United**	42	10	16	16	35	46	36	0.76
19	Sheffield Wednesday	42	12	11	19	51	63	35	0.81
20	Crystal Palace	42	11	12	19	43	56	34	0.77
21	Preston North End *	42	9	14	19	40	62	31	0.65
22	Swindon Town	42	7	11	24	36	72	25	0.50

* Deducted one point for fielding an ineligible player

UNITED'S first season in the top flight ended with them needing to beat Arsenal in the final game to stay up, a result achieved with goals from John Aldridge (penalty), Ray Houghton, and Billy Hamilton.

		P	W	D	L	F	A	Pts	GD
18	**Oxford United**	42	10	12	20	62	80	42	-18
19	Leicester City	42	10	12	20	54	76	42	-22
20	Ipswich Town	42	11	8	23	32	55	41	-23
21	Birmingham City	42	8	5	29	30	73	29	-43
22	West Bromwich Albion	42	4	12	26	35	89	24	-54

THE following season safety was secured with the penultimate game of the season, a 3-2 win at Luton Town, thanks to goals from Trevor Hebberd and two from Dean Saunders, including one in the last minute. The final game of the season, a 0-0 draw with Leicester City, condemned the Foxes to the drop.

		P	W	D	L	F	A	Pts	GD
18	**Oxford United**	42	11	13	18	44	69	46	-25
19	Charlton Athletic	42	11	11	20	45	55	44	-10
20	Leicester City	42	11	9	22	54	76	42	-22
21	Manchester City	42	8	15	19	36	57	39	-21
22	Aston Villa	42	8	12	22	45	79	36	-34

JOHNNY GOALRUSH

THE £78,000 signing of John Aldridge from Newport County in March 1984 proved to be one of the bargains of the decade. United signed Aldridge after First Division Sunderland were unable to meet Newport's asking price. After scoring in his first start, a 5-0 win over Bolton Wanderers, Aldo went on to score 90 in 141 appearances, giving him the best goals-to-games ratio of any United striker. In his first full season, Aldridge smashed the club's league goalscoring record of 24, set the previous season by Steve Biggins, with 34 goals as United stormed straight through Division Two and into the top flight. Aldridge's partnership with Billy Hamilton is still thought by many to be United's best-ever strikeforce. The higher standard of opposition proved no barrier for Aldridge, who scored 31 goals, including against his hometown team Liverpool in a 2-2 draw at the Manor, a hat-trick in a 4-3 win against Ipswich Town after Oxford were 3-0 down, and both goals in the 2-2 draw in the Milk Cup semi-final first leg at Villa Park. In 1986/87 Aldridge scored 21 goals in 30 games before his £750,000 dream move to Liverpool. His last game for Oxford was a 3-1 defeat by Watford, but it was his previous performance, in a 3-0 FA Cup defeat at Aldershot, where he was substituted for David Leworthy, that gave a clear indication that he was ready to move. Aldridge's goals were a key element in Oxford's 'Glory Years', and he will always remain a United legend.

NO EASY GAMES IN EUROPEAN FOOTBALL

THE U's aren't the only team to have represented Oxford United in Europe. *Raging Bull*, the Yellows' fanzine side, visited the village of Byaga, Bulgaria in the summer of 1991 to play Fourth Division side Bessepara FC. The Bessepara captain had won a cap for Bulgaria, and the right winger had played for Bulgaria under-21s. The villagers thought that they were playing Oxford United's reserves, and a crowd of 400 paid to watch the game in which, true to form, Bessepara went 1-0 up in the first couple of minutes. The unfit boozers of the fanzine rallied, and conceded just once more before half-time. In the second half Bessepara stopped showboating and started scoring, but goals from Will Jacobs and Will Helsby made the final score an almost respectable 9-2.

EASY GAMES IN EUROPEAN FOOTBALL

IN addition to their unsuccessful trip to Bulgaria, the *Raging Bull* team also visited Belgium in February 1992 to play supporters of Beveren. An Ian Davies goal earned the Oxford supporters a 1-0 win. *Raging Fever*, the continuation of the *Raging Bull* team formed when they combined with the *Yellow Fever* fanzine team, also visited Belgium. In April 2008 they visited Namur to play their supporters' team and won 3-0 with goals from Russell McSweeney and two from Rob Muskett. In October 2009 the Namur side visited Oxford for the rematch, but were soundly beaten 5-1, with Gez Foster scoring twice, John Matthews, James Longshaw, and an own goal completing the scoring.

SELECTION BY ELECTION

UNITED'S first application to join the Football League was made in 1952, but the club failed to receive any votes. In 1953, despite winning the Southern League and cup double, Headington still failed to get any votes, but the club applied again in 1954 after their excellent FA Cup run, and this time received their first vote, from Cardiff as thanks for Cliff Nugent. In 1955 United received two votes, but the following season they again drew a blank, although in 1958 Headington again got two votes. Another application was made in 1959 but, as before, the club was hampered by the league clubs not knowing the location of Headington and they received just seven votes. In 1960, after the club had changed its name to Oxford United, they received 10 votes at the league meeting at the Café Royal, but Peterborough United of the Midland League won 35 votes and were elected to the league in place of Gateshead, who received 18 votes. The following year, having won the Southern League, United received 19 votes, more than any of the other non-league sides, but that was still 23 fewer than Hartlepools, the lowest league side seeking re-election. However, in March 1962 Accrington Stanley resigned from the Football League, facing bankruptcy after playing 33 matches, meaning that there would be a spare place in Division Four the next season. At the Football League's annual meeting on June 2nd, Oxford, who were widely regarded as the best side not in the league, received 39 votes, more than all the other 25 non-league clubs combined (Wigan Athletic came fifth with five votes).

SEEING DOUBLE

WHEN winning the Southern League in 1952/53, Headington completed the double over seven of their opponents. They improved on this in 1960/61, when the newly named Oxford United beat nine of their opponents both home and away, a feat that the Southern League champions repeated the following season as a prelude to election to the Football League. Folkestone, and Gravesend & Northfleet, both fell victim to the U's double curse in both seasons. The 1971/72 season was the first in which United failed to complete any doubles, a record which wasn't repeated until 1987/88. In both 1998/99, and the following season, United again failed to double any of their opponents, as was the case in their relegation season to the Conference. Even in their first season in the top flight, the U's completed doubles over both Chelsea and Manchester City. Conversely, in United's first season in the Southern League they fell victim to seven doubles, a record that wasn't beaten until 1999/00, when eight sides beat the U's both home and away. Gillingham did the double over United on both occasions. Things got worse in 2000/01 when 13 sides did the double over Oxford; that's over half of United's league opponents that season. Although no-one completed the double over Headington in 1953/54, the purple patch was at the end of that decade when the U's went three seasons without being doubled: 1959/60 to 1961/62. Recently, the U's remained undoubled in 2008/09.

ALAS SMITH AND JONES

UNSURPRISINGLY, since 1949 there have been more Smiths plying their trade with United than any other surname. Andy, Barry, Charlie, Dave, Jay, Jim, Ken, and Roy Smith comprise the eight players so named, compared with six Clarkes (Bradie, Colin, Derek, James, Ryan, and Tony), four Evanses (Bernard, Ceri, and two Pauls), four Jacksons (Darren, Elliot, Fred, Jimmy), four Joneses (Davy, G. H, Mark, Tony), four Phillipses (Jimmy, Les, Lionel, Marcus), and four Thomases (Andy, Johnnie, Kevin, Martin).

CONFERENCE BOUND

WHEN Nick Merry became Oxford's chairman and installed Jim Smith as manager, United were 19th in League Two, four points above the relegation zone. A win against Peterborough United in Smith's first game back left the bottom of the table looking like this:

		P	W	D	L	F	A	Pts	GD
16	Rochdale	37	12	9	16	57	59	45	-2
17	Macclesfield Town	38	10	15	13	50	59	45	-9
18	**Oxford United**	39	10	15	14	37	47	45	-10
19	Stockport County	38	9	16	13	49	66	43	-17
20	Bury	38	10	12	16	37	49	42	-12
21	Barnet	38	9	15	14	37	50	42	-13
22	Torquay United	38	9	12	17	42	60	39	-18
23	Rushden & Ds	39	9	11	19	38	64	38	-26
24	Chester City	36	9	10	17	43	52	37	-9

ON the final day of the season, with Oxford at home to Leyton Orient, who needed a win to ensure automatic promotion, this was the scenario:

17	Bury	45	12	16	17	43	55	52	-12
18	Macclesfield Town	45	11	18	16	57	69	51	-12
19	Torquay United	45	13	12	20	53	66	51	-13
20	Barnet	45	11	18	16	42	56	51	-14
21	Notts County	45	12	15	18	46	61	51	-15
22	Stockport County	45	11	18	16	57	78	51	-21
23	**Oxford United**	45	11	16	18	41	54	49	-13
24	Rushden & Ds	45	11	12	22	43	74	45	-31

WITH Notts County at home to Bury, a win for the U's would guarantee their survival whatever the results were elsewhere. However, former United striker Lee Steele scored Orient's winning goal in the final minute to complete a 3-2 scoreline and condemn Oxford to non-league football for the first time since they were elected to the Football League 44 years earlier.